JACOB'S LADDER

To Beryl.
Many thanks for your interest.
Bob.

Bob Wragg

The moving story of the mercy killing of a terminally ill boy

Published by Albion Press
54 Hollingdean Road,
Brighton, BN2 4AA

ISBN 978-0-9558103-3-6

Printed in Great Britain by
One Digital, Brighton

For George

About the Author

Bob Wragg was born in Hertfordshire in 1941 and lived in Harpenden until his early teens when his family moved to Southampton. On leaving school he spent two years as a crew member on a research ship in Antarctica. He then joined the Metropolitan Police serving in uniform for two years, east and south London and New Scotland Yard for ten years. He was Security Manager for three national retail companies and a hotel chain before joining Cunard as Security Petty Officer on the QE2. On leaving the sea Bob was appointed Branch Manager of a national Driving School and also qualified as a driving instructor specialising in teaching disabled people to drive.

Bob has been married to Anne for 45 years and they have four children and five grandchildren. He lives in Worthing, West Sussex. His hobbies include writing, reading and watching most sports.

Acknowledgements

This book could not have been written without the help, support and backing of many people, far too many to mention, but heartfelt thanks must go to the following;-

To Steve and Carmen, Chris and Sara, Tina and Max for all their love and support. Also our extended family and friends, many of whom we had not been in touch with for some years.

Nev and Tricia in Australia, our friends in America, South Africa and Germany, too many to mention all of them personally, but whose love and encouragement to Andy, Anne and me was so appreciated.

A special thank-you to my sister Christine and her family, also Geoff and Pauline and all our extended family who gave so much support throughout. Also to Anne's family.

To our neighbours, all the staff at Goring Hall Hospital where Anne works, especially Paul and Brenda Murray (something about a kilt!), for their love and fundraising efforts – they managed to keep Anne laughing even during the dark days. Also my great friend John Bright who always believed in Andy.

To Christine Lavery MBE from the MPS Society for her advice and support, Lesley-Anne Lloyd for her tremendous encouragement in our fundraising for Chestnut Tree Children's Hospice. Also thank you to Judith Best for professional support and kindness during the two trials and the help she gave me regarding the history of Lewes Crown Court.

We will always be grateful to Vicki Hammel, who flew over from Boston to conduct Jacob's Memorial Service and burial. The counselling she gave to Andy helped him so much.

A very special thanks to Steve and Jacqui Home who so kindly allowed me to use part of the newspaper interview about their beloved son Matthew, like Jacob a Hunter Syndrome sufferer. Sadly Matthew died in October 2008. I am sure his family and all who knew him will have many wonderful memories of him and I wish them a happy future.

Also, Cathy North at Worthing Hospital, whose book about her little daughter, Zoe, gave me so much inspiration.

Thank you to Dr Eduard Verhagen of the University Medical Centre Groningen, Holland, for his information regarding euthanasia in the Netherlands.

We will always be grateful to Andy's legal team, particularly Mr Michael Sayers, QC, and Ms Louise Colwell, who were so professional but sympathetic and understanding. Also Jenny Chandler of Marten Walsh Cherer Ltd for allowing me to reprint a large part of their official trial transcripts.

A special mention to James Whale who, although he doesn't know it, gave me the original inspiration and encouragement to write the book when I spoke to him back in December 2005 and to Louise Dixon for her help and professional input.

Last but not least – even although they represent the press! – Paul Holden and Ed Mitchell for their friendship and advice in our dealings with the press and media.

The love and support of many, many people, members of the public, some of whom we never knew, carried Anne and myself through those sad, dreadful days following our grandson's death and our son's trials.

Thank you, we can never repay you all.

Finally, to my wonderful wife Anne. Only you know the many emotions I experienced in writing this book. Thankyou for your love and support – and the cups of coffee !

Preface

While he was sleeping, Jacob had a dream. In his dream he saw some stairs which led from his pillow up into the sky. There was a bright light shining on the stairway and climbing up and down the stairs were many angels. Then he dreamed that God was standing beside him telling him that wherever he went, God would be with him and take care of him.

Genesis 28:10-17

This is the story of the life of Jacob, my grandson, who suffered for ten years with a terminal illness. His father, our son, Andrew, was charged with murdering Jacob in what was described at his trial as a 'mercy killing'. When Jacob died it was generally accepted by the medical people that Jacob was nearing the end of his life.

What brought about such a tragic end for Jacob? What could have happened during his short life that affected, not only him but his dad, his mum and others so much that it ended in such a dreadful but peaceful tragedy?

This story is not all sad, because it is primarily about Jacob – and Jacob was happy, always happy. The one emotion he was able to show more than any other through all his suffering was 'happiness'. Although it is partly about people's lives being torn apart, it is also a story of deep love and the many forms it can take. It tells of two people and their remarkable lives bringing up a little boy who they knew would not live into his teens.

It will be difficult to read this story without being judgemental; I have tried not to be in writing it. It is a record of events as I remember them but I have given my opinion where I felt it necessary, I feel I am entitled to that. Not everyone will agree, and I respect their views. Many people, including my wife Anne and I, have been terribly hurt by these events and it is not my intention to add to that hurt. Perhaps, as you read this, you should remember the saying, 'there but for the grace of God go I', and ask yourself how you would cope with so much pressure under these circumstances.

I have written this book for three reasons. Firstly, in memory of Jacob. Of course he will never be forgotten; however, we are determined that he should be remembered for what he was – a beautiful grandson whom we loved so much; a remarkable little lad who touched and changed the lives of all who knew him. If, after reading this book, those who did not know Jacob feel their lives have been touched in some small way, then the memory of our grandson will be enhanced.

Secondly, it is written for Jacob's younger brother, George, who was six years old when Jacob died and who one day, perhaps, will read this and realize what a wonderful older brother he had in the early years of his life, and the contribution he himself made to Jacob's life. I hope that he will have some happy childhood memories of the fun he shared with his brother.

The events surrounding Jacob's death were headline news in the UK and reported on worldwide. Some of the newspaper and magazine articles were blatantly untrue and I considered them appalling and likely to upset George should he read them, which he surely will, when he gets older. I have thus tried to be as accurate as possible in my recollections, not only for the reader, but for George, in the hope that in the future he will not be judgemental with either of his parents, who love him dearly.

Thirdly, I have written the book as a form of therapy and in order to try to put into perspective the incidents in our lives that culminated in those dreadful days that began for Anne and me on 25 July 2004. Because of the events at the end of Jacob's life it seemed we had little time to grieve properly for him as, naturally, our lives and thoughts were dominated by Andrew's predicament and pending trial. It has been a wonderful but at times very difficult and painful journey. In writing, I have found my way of grieving for Jacob and finally coming to terms with his death, also of understanding and being more tolerant of other peoples' feelings during such traumatic times. I now realize that Jacob has changed my outlook on life and I hope I am a better person for it.

I am an emotional person and not ashamed to cry when either sad or happy. Anne and I have recalled the events from memory, my diaries, press cuttings and the like. While writing, tears have often rolled down my cheeks not only when recording sad events but also when remembering the many happy times we shared with our beloved grandson. It is intended to be a tribute to Jacob from his Nannie and Grandad.

This is our story. I have been criticized by some for writing it, even prior to publication, an opinion to which they are entitled, but I only ask that all who read the book will come to understand my reasons for doing so. Some harsh criticism even caused me to question what I was doing and I thought of stopping the project on more than one occasion. However, the memory of our beloved Jacob encouraged me to carry on and I am determined that our memories of him will not be forgotten and shared with others who were not lucky enough to know him.

Andy had no input into this book but is happy with its contents and the way I have recorded events.

Many people's lives have been changed forever, particularly those of Jacob's parents, Andy and Mary, and one can only hope that the future brings them the peace and happiness that they deserve.

Remember as you read on, despite the fact that he was in pain for much of his life but did not understand it, and despite his bad days, Jacob's aura was rarely sad. Jacob couldn't do 'sad'. Jacob could only do 'HAPPY'.

Chapter 1
It Wasn't Meant to be Like This

Sunday 25 July 2004, a date my family will remember for the rest of our lives. It was 5.15 a.m. I must have been in a deep sleep because I didn't hear the doorbell ring. Anne, a lighter sleeper, did, and answered the door.

'Bob! Wake up!' she shook me awake. 'There's a policeman at the door and he wants to speak to us.'

I put on my dressing-gown as I went downstairs and my first thoughts were the same as Anne's. 'Oh no, it's one of the children. Have they been involved in an accident?' Before my thoughts raced on any more I was facing the police officer at the front door. He was not in uniform and introduced himself to us as he showed his identity. I presumed he was in the CID. Anne was standing behind me.

'Good morning, Mr Wragg, I'm sorry to disturb you at this time of the night but I'm afraid I have some bad news. It's Jacob. I am sorry to have to tell you that he's dead.'

When you are waiting for tragic news that you know will come eventually there still seems no way to prepare for it: the shock still hits you in the pit of the stomach. The police officer waited a few seconds for Anne and me to absorb what he'd said, but then continued, 'I'm afraid it's not just that. Can I come in?'

We knew that Jacob had a terminal illness; we knew that he was poorly; and we knew that he was going to die. We were expecting this sad news sooner rather than later. But why is a police officer coming round to tell us this? And a CID officer at that? Surely it would be Andy or Mary who would eventually give us the news that the suffering Jacob had endured for the past ten years was finally at an end? We all sat down in our sitting room.

'Mr and Mrs Wragg, I am sorry to have to tell you that Jacob died earlier tonight and Andy, your son, and his wife, Mary, have been arrested on suspicion of his murder.'

Anne and I were sitting together on the settee. We looked at each other, put our arms around one another and both started to cry. I don't honestly remember what we said, things like 'Oh, my God, no! It can't be true!' I suppose. How do you remember such trivial things when your whole mind and being have been shot into turmoil?

I do recall asking the officer what happened and he told us he was unable to give any details other than that Andy was at Chichester Police Station and Mary was at Worthing. He said we could not visit or speak to them at present but we would be informed of any developments. I asked about George, Jacob's younger brother, and was relieved to hear that he was with Gwen, Mary's mother.

After the officer had gone, Anne and I sat down for a few minutes, trying to gather our thoughts, but things had to be done. It was 5.30 a.m. How does anyone make rational decisions at that time of the day – particularly when you have just been told your grandson is dead and his father and mother have been arrested for his murder?

I decided to phone Chris, my youngest son, and his wife, Sara. This was the first of many phone calls I had to make, and no matter how hard I tried it didn't get easier. Anne was very supportive though. When I broke down during the phone calls she would take over, hard as it was for her, but we had to tell our family and close friends what had happened, although we knew very little at the time. Chris and Sara came straight down to Worthing from their home in Wimbledon and I asked Chris to bring some clothes with him so that we could give them to Andy, as I knew the police would have taken his from him when he was arrested. My daughter Tina, her husband, Max, and their daughter, Ella, live not far from us and we went round to their house at about seven o'clock that morning to tell them. I phoned my eldest son, Steve, and his wife, Carmen, who live in America. I didn't think about the time difference and I broke the news to them just as they were getting ready for bed. Poor things, I realized as soon as I had rung off that they wouldn't get any sleep that night, waiting for news from us back at home.

I phoned Mary's mum and she confirmed that George was with her. She lives in a flat not far from Andy and Mary's home. I asked her if she knew what had happened. She said she didn't but added, 'Mary came round with George at about 11.10 last night. She was very upset. I couldn't make much sense of what she was saying. She was, well, more or less hysterical and she whispered to me, "It's Jacob, we've got problems. Can you look after George?" Of course I said I would.' Gwen went on to tell me that she knew no more than that Jacob was dead and Andy and Mary were in custody. I told her that Anne and I would be happy to have George stay with us if it would help but she had already spoken to her other daughter, Ann, and that George was going to stay with her for a few days. Their only immediate problem was that George had no clothes or toys with him, because Mary had dropped him off in his pyjamas and the police would not let anyone go back into the family home. Gwen said she and Ann would go to town and buy things for George.

At about 9.15 a.m. Detective Constable Dowell, the Family Liaison Officer, came to see us. Over the next few days we saw him and spoke to him on the phone quite a few times. He was pleasant and seemed sympathetic, considering the circumstances. However, being an ex-police officer myself, I know how difficult it can be dealing with the family of a person you or your colleagues have just arrested for murder. Although he was a Family Liaison Officer and explained that he had nothing to do with the investigation of Jacob's death, I was fully aware that anything Anne or I said to the detriment of Mary or Andy would be relayed back to the investigating officers – not that we had any information regarding Jacob's death.

He accepted the offer of a cup of coffee and we sat down, Anne and me next to each other, holding hands tightly. He asked us if we knew what had happened and we told him we didn't, other than what the officer who called to break the news had told us. DC Dowell continued, 'It appears that at about eleven o'clock last night Mary took George round to Gwen's and dropped him off. When she returned to her home Andy was there. He had smothered Jacob with a pillow. The paramedics were called and tried to revive Jacob. They couldn't and wanted to take him to hospital. Mary was absolutely hysterical and didn't want them to take him. She just wanted to be left alone with him. She had to be restrained and was arrested because of her behaviour, basically to prevent a breach of the peace. She is in custody in Worthing and Andy in Chichester, both on suspicion of murder.'

So we now knew the stark facts, at least the 'police version' of them, which we had no reason to doubt.

Anne and I put our arms around each other and cried. I honestly don't know what I was thinking or saying for the next few minutes, Anne says she doesn't remember either. That's what shock does to you, I guess. I do know that most of my thoughts were about Andy our son, and Mary, of course, but Andy is our flesh and blood. I suppose the expression 'blood is thicker than water' must mean there is always an unbreakable, subconscious bond between parents and children.

What about Jacob though? Yes, of course we were weeping for him as well but on reflection, from early that Sunday morning, we were robbed of the chance of grieving Jacob's passing. It was true that over the previous few months, because of his state of health, Anne and I, and I am sure many others, had thought about Jacob's inevitable death. Had he died naturally, we would, obviously, have grieved and mourned our loss but we would also have felt a sense of relief that the little boy was finally at rest and his suffering and pain had come to an end. This news changed all that. Yes, Jacob was now finally at peace, for which we were grateful, but our son and daughter-in-law were sitting in police cells suspected of his murder. What should we be thinking? This wasn't how it should have been. We hadn't planned for this.

The one crumb of comfort, if you can call it that, was that DC Dowell informed us that when he was arrested Andy had told the police that 'it was a mercy killing' and he 'loved Jacob so much'. During the various conversations we had with DC Dowell he said that of course at this early stage he was unable to predict an outcome, however, his own personal opinion, not speaking as a police officer, was that because of the tragic circumstances, Andy and Mary should not be charged. Although that was his view, I at no time believed or thought that there would not be charges made against either Andy or Mary or both. After all, Jacob was dead. Andy had evidently told the police what he had done and the law has to take its course, just or otherwise. My twelve years' experience in the Metropolitan Police taught me that the law does not always appear to be fair. However, in a civilized society, the law must be upheld and when it is not then, following investigation, prosecution may or may not follow. The police are not judge and jury, it is their duty to put the facts to the Crown Prosecution Service who make the decision whether to prosecute or not.

When he was taken into custody, Andy had elected to appoint the Duty Solicitor to represent him. Mr Oscar Vincent from Edward Hayes Solicitors advised Andy to say nothing when he was interviewed by the police in the several interviews that took place at Chichester Police Station.

That evening, brief facts appeared on both the BBC and ITV for the first time. Pictures of Andy's house, taped off as a crime scene, were shown. Over the next three days more news was reported on television and radio and it very soon became obvious that many friends and acquaintances had seen it. Anne and I started to get cards, letters and phone calls from people we hadn't seen or heard from for many years. The circumstances of Jacob's death had been reported virtually worldwide and over the next few days we received phone calls from friends in Australia, the USA, South Africa and Germany. Letters arrived from everywhere, about 150, and every single one came with love and support not just for Anne and me but for Andy, Mary and all our family. It was reported that Jacob had been attending Chestnut Tree Children's Hospice in Worthing, and several people with whom we had lost contact up to forty years ago wrote to us via the Hospice. I think Anne and I eventually replied, either by letter or phone, to everyone who was kind enough to write – we certainly tried to. Later, Andy read all the cards and letters and was touched by the support they conveyed.

By Monday morning we were inundated by the press, both national and local. Anne and I were very relieved that our son Chris, a television sports producer, and his wife Sara, an author and award-winning journalist, were with us. They handled all the members of the press who called at the house in a very firm but polite manner. The press obviously have a job to do, I understand that, and at this stage they were not overly intrusive. Their reports as they appeared over the next few days were one hundred per cent sympathetic towards Andy.

Late on the Monday evening, Andy and Mary appeared, separately, at Chichester Magistrates' Court before a specially convened Bench of Lay Magistrates. The police asked for a further forty-eight hours in which to keep them in custody and question them. The magistrates granted a thirty-six hour extension. We were still not allowed to see Andy or Mary.

The following day two CID officers came to the house to interview Anne and me. I knew from my police experience exactly why they had come and what they wanted. I felt that neither Anne nor I could or would be material witnesses to poor Jacob's actual death. We had talked briefly to the officer who had first broken the news to us and we had also spoken to DC Dowell in general terms about the way we had seen Jacob's health deteriorate recently. However, I knew that these two officers were part of the investigation team and they would want any information we were willing to give them about such things as Andy and Mary's relationship, how they treated the boys, etc. I also knew that once either of us said anything to the police that might be remotely of interest to them, they would want to take a written statement. The significance of that, if we agreed, was that we could be called as witnesses for the prosecution and, furthermore, we could not then be interviewed by Andy's solicitor. So Anne and I both politely informed the two officers that anything we had to say would be to Andy's solicitor, and they said they fully understood. It was not a case of obstructing the police – that is quite a different matter – we just wanted to help our son in any way we could.

That evening, DC Dowell phoned to tell us that Andy had been charged with Jacob's murder and that Mary had been released without charge. Naturally Anne and I were upset at the news that Andy had been charged but it was not unexpected, and it was a relief that Mary was free to comfort and look after George. DC Dowell told us that we could now visit Andy in the Custody Suite at Chichester. Following DC Dowell's phone call, Chris and I drove immediately to Mary's house. She had been picked up from the police station by her sister, Ann, and they arrived at the house just as we did. As one might expect of someone who has spent three days being questioned about the alleged murder of her son, Mary looked awful, and she was obviously upset. Understandably, she wanted to enter the house alone, so Ann, Chris and I stood outside for a short time talking in the rain. Mary seemed quite concerned because, on the advice of his solicitor, Andy had said nothing to the police during interview. She asked me to tell Andy to consider changing his solicitor. I didn't know the reason for Mary's concern and I found it strange, as it is quite usual for an arrested person to take the advice of his solicitor and say nothing when questioned by the police. I told Mary that I would tell Andy of her concerns, but I felt he was getting good legal advice. We told Mary we were going to try and visit Andy that night although it was late and she said, 'When you see him, tell him I love him.'

Chris and I picked Anne up and we drove to Chichester to visit Andy in the Police Custody Suite. He had given up smoking some months previously but his solicitor had told me on the phone that he had started again. Given the predicament he was in it was hardly surprising and so we stopped at an all-night garage and bought him some cigarettes. We arrived at the Custody Suite at about 12.45 a.m. It is a new-looking building that looks from the outside like a health club or fitness centre, and it is staffed mainly by a private security company. We were met by a female security officer. She politely told us that we would not be able to see Andy because they were 'short-staffed'. It was a bitter disappointment, particularly as we had had no contact with Andy since his arrest. The officer was sympathetic but told us that Andy was bearing up remarkably well and had spent a long time with his solicitor. We handed over his cigarettes and Chris's clothing for him to wear in court later that morning. The officer promised to give him our love and we left.

On the Wednesday morning, Anne decided that the ordeal of the court hearing would be too much for her and that she would stay home: Chris, Sara, Tina and I all felt that that was the correct decision. But even before we left the house to attend court, three members of the press called at the door, and while we were actually in court another two were politely told by our neighbour to respect our privacy. Quite rightly, Anne did not answer the door to them. Outside the court we had to run the gauntlet of numerous national and local press, TV and radio reporters, but we said nothing to them.

Andy was brought from the Custody Centre to the rear entrance of the court in a prison van and the media were waiting. Andy later told me that he was asked by one of the escorting officers if he wanted to put a blanket over his head so that the press could not take any pictures of him. He declined, telling them that he had done nothing to be ashamed of.

Before the hearing we met Andy's solicitor for the first time and he told us that he would inform the Magistrates of Andy's intention to plead not guilty to the charge of murder. He implied that a lesser charge of 'manslaughter on the grounds of diminished responsibility' might be the eventual outcome, but nothing could be guaranteed. I was pleased to hear that even at this early stage it was being considered.

I guess that for Tina, Chris and Sara, seeing the inside of a court for the first time, it would have a lasting effect on them. I have given evidence in many Magistrates' Courts, Crown Courts and the No. 1 Court at the Old Bailey – indeed, giving evidence in court was one of my favourite parts of police work and I never really suffered from nerves. However, sitting in that court waiting for my son to appear in the dock was probably the most heartbreaking, stomach-churning, feeling I have ever experienced.

That memory will remain with me for the rest of my life.

We, the public, sat immediately opposite the magistrates' bench, with the lawyers in the middle. The dock, which seemed to be vast, was to our right and about halfway down the courtroom. It was completely surrounded by glass and there was a door at the back from which the prisoners entered. The press bench was next to the dock. I held Tina's hand and Chris held Sara's. Andy's friends sat behind us and it was obvious that everyone else in the court was looking at us for any signs of emotion we might show.

The three magistrates entered, we all stood, the clerk and lawyers bowed to them and we all sat. The clerk's voice rang round the courtroom, 'Put up Andrew Wragg.'

The door at the back of the dock opened and Andy entered, flanked by two Security Officers. This was the first time any of us had seen Andrew since his arrest. He looked around the court and quickly saw us, giving a slight nod of the head in acknowledgement. I returned the gesture. Our son looked ashen-faced and shocked.

'Are you Andrew Wragg?' enquired the clerk.

'Yes.'

'Mr Wragg, the charge against you is that on Saturday 24th July 2004, at Henty Close, Worthing, you murdered Jacob Wragg. Do you understand?'

'Yes.'

Andy was then told to sit. His lawyer informed the bench that he was representing Andrew. A female lawyer outlined the prosecution case, explaining to the magistrates that Jacob was suffering from a terminal genetic disorder and that on Saturday night his mother, Mary, had taken his brother, George, to Mary's mother's for the night. When she returned home she found her husband Andrew with Jacob, who appeared collapsed. Jacob was taken to hospital by ambulance but pronounced dead. The police had been called and Andrew allegedly admitted to them that he had smothered Jacob with a pillow. The lawyer went on to say that it was a very sad case. I gripped Tina's hand and we were both crying. I looked at Chris and Sara and they both had tears streaming down their faces. Andy was sitting in the dock with his head bowed staring at the floor. Mr Vincent stood up and informed the bench that he was not applying for bail on behalf of his client but that he would be doing so at the next court appearance. He had already explained to us that he had not had sufficient time to prepare a strong application but he was hopeful that bail might be granted at the next hearing. It is quite rare for anyone charged with murder to be granted bail; however, this was a very unusual case. Oscar Vincent further informed the court that he anticipated Andrew would be pleading not guilty to the charge of murder.

Andy was remanded in custody until 5 August, when he would appear at Lewes Crown Court. As he was led away, he turned, looked across and raised his hand in acknowledgement of us. I gave him a thumbs-up sign, hoping to convey the support and love that we all felt for him. We were not allowed to visit Andy in the cells.

The police informed us that the press and TV cameras were desperate to get pictures and quotes and they were gathered in their hordes on the court steps. We agreed that Andy's solicitor would make a short statement to the reporters on behalf of Andy and the family, asking them to respect our privacy. As he did so, the police escorted Chris, Sara, Tina and me to our cars, accompanied all the way by photographers and reporters. I suppose they were as respectful as they could be, given that they have a job to do. We returned to Worthing to be told by Anne that there had already been reports on the television news.

We all felt completely drained by the day's events and agreed that the sight of Andy standing in the dock was a shattering, heartbreaking experience. Anne said that she would go to future court hearings to show love and support for Andy, no matter how hard she found it. We discussed prison visits and various other matters but the sad thing, on reflection, is that we hardly talked about Jacob. At a time when we should all have been grieving our loss, our thoughts were consumed by Andy's predicament. How could we not think of him in prison? What was his mental state, knowing that he had ended Jacob's life?

It took a little while for Anne and me to realize that we had been robbed of the grieving process, and would be for some time. Anne and I have never taken tranquillizers or sleeping tablets and despite the fact that, even now, we find sleep difficult, we have coped. A few days after Jacob's death I got up at 4.30 a.m. and there on the television news was a picture of Jacob and of us all leaving court. Reports and pictures of Andy were in the national papers. All our lives seemed to have been consumed by the events and there was no escaping it.

Chapter 2
The Family

Andrew was born on 8 August 1967 at the Memorial Hospital, Shooters Hill in south London. He is our second eldest son, Stephen having been born two years earlier. At the time I was a detective in the Metropolitan Police and Anne was a State Registered nurse.

Three years later we had our daughter, Joanne, so we had the perfect family – two boys and a beautiful baby girl – and Anne and I decided that we did not want more children. But our world was shattered in March 1971 when Joanne, just six and a half months old, became seriously ill, was rushed to hospital, and died of pneumonia during the night. Although she had suffered a severe chest infection three months earlier, we'd thought she was fully recovered and did not realize the devastating effect it had left on her lungs.

Anyone who has experienced the death of a baby will know the dreadful effect it has on a family. I will never forget the feelings I had the following morning, knowing that I had to tell Steve and Andy that their little sister had died and gone to heaven. Steve, being that little bit older, seemed to understand more than Andy, and I vividly remember driving Anne and the boys to Worthing to break the sad news to Anne's family.

At one point Andy suddenly said to me, 'Daddy, you said Joanne has gone to heaven and it is a nice place and Jesus is looking after her?'

'Yes, that's right, Andy,' I replied.

'Well, why does everyone keep crying then? We should be happy.'

I can't remember what I said in reply, I just remember giving him a hug and choking back the tears. Anne and I tried so hard to carry on with our lives at that time and make everything as normal as possible for the sake of the boys, but what with the funeral and so on, it was difficult. We had no counselling, it wasn't on offer in those days.

Because of the course that Andy's life has taken, it has been suggested that perhaps one of the many contributory factors might have been the effect that Joanne's death, and the way Anne and I handled it, had on him. We decided that neither of the boys should come to the funeral, for instance. Perhaps they should have had the chance to say their 'goodbyes'. Who knows? Hindsight is a wonderful thing.

Anne and I always remember Joanne's birthday and put some fresh flowers in the house on that day each year. When Steve and Andy lived at home we included them and reminded them of their little baby sister. Even in her short life she has left us with happy memories and, as with Jacob, we will never forget her beautiful big smile.

Christopher, our third son, was born in January 1973 and, in May 1974, our darling daughter Christina was born. Life is so strange, the death of little Joanne resulted in us having two more wonderful children. Chris was the only one of our children to attend university where he gained an MA degree and has followed a successful career in the sports media. Tina is an equine veterinary nurse and a working mum.

Shortly after Tina arrived I left the police force and we moved, first to Southampton and later to Worthing. Over the next few years the children grew up and had what they have told me was a happy childhood. Steve and Andy were very much a pair. Steve is a pragmatist and can invariably be relied upon to offer a well thought-through evaluation of most situations. Andy has always been the joker in the pack. Deep down he is emotional but he seems frightened of showing it. In some ways I suppose he can be described as 'a bit of a loner', which he agrees with. He can be very funny sometimes but serious and solemn at others. As he has grown older he has kept his thoughts to himself and never really opened up or completely confided in us, but he has his own way of showing his love. I was later to see a very emotional and loving side to his character.

My family are the epitome of a close-knit loving family, and Jacob's life – and death – have further cemented that. His life, his suffering, the happiness he radiated and his passing have brought us so close – yet another legacy from our little grandson.

Andy, Steve and I have a small claim to fame in that all three of us have been to Antarctica. In 1959, aged eighteen, I spent two years as a crew member on the Research Ship *John Biscoe* with the British Antarctic Survey. From November 1983 to June 1984, Andy followed in my footsteps as a member of the crew of the Research Ship *Bransfield,* which by that time had replaced the *Biscoe.* I was so proud of him as he was only sixteen. Steve served on the *Bransfield* from 1984, after Andy had left, to 1985. Both boys had fantastic experiences, as I had previously, visiting such places as Rio, the Falklands and South Georgia, not to mention the breathtaking sites of frozen Antarctica. Andy and Steve left home as teenagers and returned as young men of character, far more independent than most men of their age.

On his return home in 1984, Andy joined the Merchant Navy Training School at Gravesend to study catering. He passed with flying colours and was awarded a prize for student of his year. On passing out, he went to sea with several shipping companies serving as a chef on tankers, cargo ships and passenger ships, including the *QE2.* I had also spent three years working on the *QE2* and my father had spent his whole life in the Merchant Navy.

It was early in the 1990s, while he was on leave in Worthing from one of his trips around the world, that Andy met Mary.

Mary was born in August 1962 and was adopted when she was a baby by two lovely people, Ron and Gwen Richards. They had already adopted another baby, Ann, who is a year or two older than Mary. The family lived in Worthing and the girls grew up and went to school there. Ron was an accountant and company secretary working for a firm in Covent Garden in London until his retirement. Sadly, he died a few years ago, after a long battle with cancer. I sometimes wonder what he would have made of the situation surrounding Jacob's death. He was a lovely man and Anne and I often had heart-to-heart talks with him and Gwen about Mary and Andy's relationship and the trauma with little Jacob. When Andy later joined the army, Ron told me he was proud of him and what he was doing for his family. I really appreciated that.

Several years ago, Mary decided to trace her birth mother. Her name is Marion and she lives in south London. Andy and Mary arranged to meet her and the reunion was evidently a tearful but happy occasion. Mary has kept in touch with Marion on a fairly regular basis since then and gets on well with her other children.

After meeting Mary, Andy stayed at sea for a few months and while on leave spent all his time with her. She later told us that one of the things that attracted her to him was his sense of humour and 'cheek'.

The first time she met him she asked him 'Would you like a drink?'

'Yes,' he replied.

'Yes what?' asked Mary.

'Yes, I would like a drink!' came the reply.

Anne and I were introduced to Mary and liked her immediately. She seemed to think the world of our son and we were happy that Andy had met someone for whom he had genuine feelings. At that time, Mary was working as deputy manager at a public house in Worthing, and after a few months Andy decided to leave the sea and join her. They passed the interviews and became relief managers for a large brewery. They worked in various pubs in the south and talked of the possibility of getting a public house of their own, if the right opportunity arose.

In 1992 the couple were managing a pub for a few weeks near Colchester, Essex. It was while they were there that Andy decided to apply to join the army, and attended the Recruitment Centre in the town.

After going through the usual selection procedures, Andy was posted to the Royal Signals Regiment and did his basic training at Catterick, Yorkshire. During that time it transpired that for Andy and Mary to be given army living quarters, they would have to be married. I think they were planning to get married sometime in the future but army regulations dictated that it should be earlier if they wanted to live together.

The wedding took place at the Worthing Registry and it was a small and low-key affair. Very few relatives from either side attended, just Anne and I, Tina, and Chris, who was best man. From Mary's family, her parents were there, also her sister with her husband and their daughter. Some of Mary and Andy's friends were invited but only two or three other relatives. A small reception, with buffet and drinks, was held in a local pub but there were no speeches. It was all arranged so quickly, I guess Andy and Mary had no choice other than to have a small, quiet wedding.

The couple returned to Catterick, Andy to complete his basic training and Mary to start a new life as an army wife. They were allocated a small but adequate house within the Catterick Garrison. A short time later, in October 1992, Andy finished his training and we all went to his Passing Out Parade. I was so proud, seeing Andy march onto that parade ground with a Regimental Band playing. Tears rolled down my cheeks and even now, writing this, I feel full of emotion.

Andy and Mary seemed to settle quickly down to army life. A signaller, Andy spent several periods away from home at various military establishments in the UK on courses connected with his trade, but Mary accepted it as part of being married to a soldier.

Then, in April 1993, Andy phoned to tell us the fantastic news that we were going to be grandparents! Anne and I were so happy for them and so proud that we were going to be grandparents for the first time. Anne busied herself with the usual things expectant grandmothers do, knitting baby clothes and crocheting a beautiful multi-coloured cot quilt. We visited Andy and Mary in Catterick during the pregnancy and, as far as we knew, Mary had no complications. They, like us and all the rest of the family, looked forward so much to the birth and I will always remember the pride in Andy's voice the day he phoned to tell us that Mary had had a routine scan and the baby was a boy.

After several months serving in the Royal Signals Regiment at Catterick, Andy was promoted to Corporal and in the autumn of 1993 decided to apply to join the elite SAS Regiment, who have a reputation for being the finest in the world. Their work is mainly covert, highly secret, carried out in theatres of war and behind enemy lines. He passed the very difficult selection procedure and then began the training at the SAS Headquarters in Hereford. It was extremely gruelling, both mentally and physically, an indication of this being that of the sixty-eight recruits who started the training with Andy, only nine finished it – the average pass rate is evidently seven per cent. Andy admitted that at times he felt like giving up – and even cried on occasions. However, the one thing that kept him going was the knowledge that what he was doing was not just to fulfil his own ambition but was also for his wife and the son they were expecting soon.

Andy later explained to us how he and Mary had chosen the name 'Jacob' for their firstborn. Part of the SAS training took place in Wales – in the Brecon Beacons – and it culminated in a fifty-five-mile trek, near the end of which was a peak called Jacob's Ladder. When the recruits finally reached that point they knew that they had nearly completed their training and it was at that time that Andy decided, if he had a son, he would name him Jacob.

Jacob was born on 23 November 1993.

Andy sounded so proud when he phoned to give us the news and assure us that mother and baby were fine. He told us of the nightmare journey to get Mary, in labour, from their home in Catterick to the hospital, several miles away. It was dark, there was thick snow and the roads were treacherous. However, they made it and Mary had a normal delivery.

On hearing the news, I remember, Anne and I were overcome with emotion and joy; we couldn't wait to see our first grandchild. Anne, Chris and I drove up to Catterick and stayed for just the one night. Little Jacob was so beautiful and seemed completely healthy.

Chris had brought Jacob a baby-sized Southampton Football Club shirt – Andy, Chris and I are keen Saints supporters – and we have a lovely photo of Chris holding Jacob and Jacob looking every bit a Junior Saint. Imagine our dismay when, for reasons known only to himself, Jacob later switched his allegiance to Chelsea!

We returned to Worthing, happy and proud grandparents and uncle, to settle back into our routine lives but looking forward to seeing plenty of our new grandson in the future. Andy returned to Hereford to continue his training, and Mary remained in Catterick with the new baby. In January 1994 Andy completed his course, was awarded the much coveted SAS beret and belt and officially became a member of the elite SAS Regiment. I could not have been more proud of him.

He was allocated a house and immediately moved Mary and Jacob from Catterick to Hereford to begin a new phase in their life. They quickly seemed to appreciate the lovely part of the country in which they were living, as we did when we visited them. Andy spent a fair amount of time away from Hereford either on various courses, during which he was awarded his parachute wings, or on special missions of which we knew nothing. He travelled to France and Cyprus, among other places. In mid-1994 Britain was engaged in the war in the Balkans and subsequently Andy was seconded to the United Nations Force in Bosnia and served there for approximately three months. I do not know what duties Andy was required to carry out during his service in Bosnia – he was, and will always be, subject to the Official Secrets Act and he has never discussed those experiences. Because of the nature of the work they do, members of the SAS have to be very secretive about their existence. He did receive the United Nations medal on completion of his tour in Bosnia, as did all military personnel who served there.

While Andy was away, Mary was on her own with Jacob in Hereford but we all made sure she was not lonely and visited them frequently. In September 1994, when Andy was still in Bosnia, Anne and I went to Hereford and spent a very enjoyable holiday with Mary and Jacob. While we were there, Mary mentioned that Jacob seemed to have a permanent cold and had been on antibiotics for some time. She discussed this with Anne and they both agreed that the amount of antibiotics Jacob had been prescribed since his birth was excessive for a baby of that age. He certainly appeared to have a constantly runny nose and, on reflection, I think Mary probably had a mother's intuition that Jacob was not as healthy as he should have been at that stage of his life. At the end of the holiday we returned to Worthing but Mary's parents went to stay with her for Jacob's first birthday. Mary put on a little party for him, which Gwen recorded on video camera. When we look at it now, it is sad to see how Jacob was on that day, he is very lethargic, not taking any interest in his surroundings and not smiling. He just looks so full of cold. However, he soon appeared to get better. Andy was due home from Bosnia and Mary drove to Brize Norton with Jacob to meet him. Andy told us that as he stepped off the plane he spotted Jacob immediately because he was wearing his Southampton shirt. Andy remained at home in Hereford for a few months and, apart from short training courses, had no long periods away.

In January 1995 Mary became pregnant again and we were all delighted that Jacob was going to have a brother or sister.

In April of that year, Andy and Mary went to the Caribbean for two weeks, the first holiday they had had since getting married. We had a glorious time looking after Jacob, and Anne kept a photo diary, which we gave to Andy and Mary when they got back. I have lovely memories of Jacob getting into bed with his Nannie each morning and me taking them breakfast in bed – he thought that was great. During his stay with us, Jacob developed a cold and breathing problems and Anne was concerned enough to take him to our GP, who thought it could be asthma related.

When they got back from holiday, Andy went to begin a course in Harrogate. Mary took Jacob to their own doctor, who sent him off for extensive investigations, tests and observations, which involved admission to Hereford hospital. As a nurse, Anne felt that cystic fibrosis could be in the equation, so we were mightily relieved when the tests proved that not to be so. The investigations continued, however, and finally, on 22 June, Mary phoned to say that Jacob was suffering from a very rare genetic disorder called mucopolysaccharidosis, MPS, also known as Hunter Syndrome. She told us that the condition was terminal.

Mucopolysaccharidosis is a group of inherited metabolic disorders in which there is an abnormality of a specific enzyme. This abnormality affects the way carbohydrates are handled within the body's cells, leading to an accumulation in the tissues of unwanted substances. With Hunter Syndrome only a female can be a carrier of the MPS genes but they will not develop the disease, whereas the male will. The features of Hunter Syndrome include abnormalities of the skeleton, central nervous system and brain, causing mental retardation. The patient has characteristic facial features, one being a prominent forehead, though this was not obvious to us when Jacob was born. Also, Hunter boys will gradually develop an enlarged liver and spleen, distended stomach and severe joint stiffness. The brain and other organs eventually 'fur up'. The life expectancy of a Hunter sufferer is between nine and twelve years, depending on the severity of the syndrome. Death is usually caused by heart attack, stroke, pneumonia, liver or kidney failure or choking. Although research is continuing, no specific treatment is available and each problem is dealt with, if possible, as it occurs. This was the prognosis given to Mary and Andy.

With hindsight, it is easy to criticize, but perhaps the doctors involved could have been more sympathetic to the situation. Mary had taken Jacob for the tests on her own, but Andy, who had been on a course, was on his way home, and Mary told the doctor this. Despite that, however, Mary was alone, with no one to comfort her, when she was given the heartbreaking news that her son had a terminal illness., The doctor, who was accompanied by several medical students, informed Mary that Jacob's was an extremely rare condition for which there was no cure. The medical staff had evidently not seen anyone with Jacob's illness before and the doctor went on to ask Mary if she would allow them to undress Jacob and take photographs of him. She quite naturally refused, feeling that she did not want her son to be seen as some kind of freak. To make matters worse, she was also told that her unborn baby might be also suffering from the same condition.

I was at work in my office and was shattered when Anne phoned me with the devastating news. We rushed to Hereford and by the time we arrived Andy had returned from Harrogate. I returned home after three days, not really understanding what the future held for all of us, but Anne stayed in Hereford giving Andy and Mary what support she could.

On 26 June, Mary went to hospital for tests to ascertain if the baby she was carrying was also suffering from MPS. By now she was just over seven months' pregnant. She was told that the results would be through in two days, but there was an agonizing wait of four days before she and Andy were called back to see the consultant. Anne stayed at their house and looked after Jacob and she told Mary and Andy to take their time and, if the news was good, she suggested they went out to lunch and spent a little time on their own. As time went on and they did not return, Anne played with Jacob and started to feel positive. Her words best convey what happened: 'I looked out of the window and saw them coming up the path. Andy saw me and gave me the "thumbs down" sign. They came into the house and Andy picked up Jacob. We all put our arms around each other and just hugged and cried. We were unable to talk.'

The consultant had explained to Andy and Mary that the baby boy they were expecting also had Hunter Syndrome and, like Jacob, would suffer all his life from its debilitating effects, probably dying before he reached his teens. They were given the option of terminating the pregnancy but were told that they had to make that decision within a matter of hours.

While Anne kept Jacob happy, Mary and Andy sat and discussed the options. Should they agree to end the seven-month pregnancy, lose their baby, but thus be able to devote the whole of their love and time to Jacob? They knew well the difficulties they faced with Jacob. Could they face the same with another son? Could they cope with watching both their sons suffer and eventually die? Their love and devotion for Jacob, they felt, was paramount, and their decision to allow the doctors to terminate Mary's pregnancy has always been totally supported by the family. I can understand those who, maybe for religious beliefs or other reasons, would disagree. However, I believe whatever decision is made by parents under such circumstances should be fully supported by their family and friends. Mary and Andy made a great sacrifice for their love of Jacob.

Late that afternoon Andy took Mary back to hospital.

On hearing of their decision, I went back to Hereford immediately to offer what support I could and help Anne look after Jacob. Tears came to my eyes several times during that journey. It's strange how certain things trigger memories. I remember it was a beautiful summer evening and I had the car windows open. I passed a field, which had obviously recently been mowed, and that beautiful smell of freshly cut grass wafted into the car. Now, each time I experience that smell, I think of Jacob.

As I approached the outskirts of Hereford, my favourite hymn, 'Abide With Me', was played on the car radio and, again, I started to cry. I am not religious but I am very emotional and that hymn always affects me. It is sung at the FA Cup Final each year and every time I hear it I recall a wonderful day, 1 May 1976, when the football team I support, Southampton, won the cup. I have many happy memories of that day out at Wembley, especially as Steve, my eldest son who was eleven at the time, was with me. Listening to that hymn and thinking that Andy would never be able experience such happy father-and-son memories with Jacob tore me apart.

In truth, I wanted to turn the car around and go home again – I thought I was in the middle of some sort of nightmare that I didn't want any part of, and that if I headed back to Worthing, then everything would be OK. Those thoughts lasted for no more than a few seconds because I knew I had to join Andy, Mary, Jacob and Anne and give them what support I could in our family tragedy.

When I arrived, Andy was back at home, having left Mary in a private room in the maternity unit. He said how sad it was that she was able to hear the crying of newly born babies. Andy put Jacob to bed and then had dinner with Anne and me. We drank two or three bottles of wine and talked late into the night. Andy didn't try to explain in detail the reasons for the distressing decision he and Mary had made just a few hours earlier. They didn't have to justify it to anyone – and I know Anne and I would have done the same. Poor Andy, he cried a lot, knowing that the life of his unborn son, whose birth he and Mary had been so looking forward to in a few weeks, was going to be clinically ended the next morning.

We were thinking of Mary. How could anyone possibly know what she must have been going through, lying in a hospital bed knowing her pregnancy was to be terminated and she had a little boy at home who had a terminal illness? Jacob awoke once during the night but soon dropped off again after Andy gave him a drink. The rest of us had little sleep that night.

The 1st of July was one of the saddest days in all our lives. Andy left early to join Mary at the hospital, while Anne and I looked after Jacob. Neither Andy nor Mary have described to us the events that took place that day but it must have been unimaginably traumatic for both of them. Mary was heavily sedated but from the witness box at his subsequent trial, Andy described in graphic detail how he was not warned by the doctors of the procedure and of watching on a screen as a long needle was put into Mary's stomach. As Andy told of the heartbreaking experience the court went silent and many, including jury members and hardened press reporters, were in tears. Andy said at least two attempts were made to locate the baby's heart, which was finally injected, ending their son's life. A few hours later, Mary gave birth to their stillborn son, Henry. Andy was with Mary to give her love and support during that terrible time but there is no doubt that it has had a lasting effect on him.

Andy later went to the hospital cafeteria and a man, whom he had seen earlier in the maternity unit and whose wife had just given birth, asked him if he had a boy or a girl. Andy told him he had a boy, but not wanting to dampen the new father's excitement, didn't say anything else. Later that day, I went to visit Mary and she took me to see baby Henry. He looked so peaceful and perfect, with a lot of hair considering he was only just over seven months old. Mary spent a lot of time with Henry and took some photographs of him before she left hospital the next day.

Steve came over from Germany and stayed with Mary and Andy for a week, Anne and I returned home, our emotions in turmoil.

The Padre of Andy's Regiment, Jimmy Morrison, gave what help and support he could during those difficult early days after Henry's death. Mary and Andy wanted a very quiet, private funeral for Henry and on 5 July he was buried in the children's section of the churchyard in Hereford. There was no church service. Andy and Mary met Jimmy at the graveside and no one else attended. Prayers were said, baby Henry was laid to rest and Mary and Andy returned home to concentrate their love on Jacob. We will not forget Henry and, although he never knew it, his premature death contributed to a loving and happy life for Jacob.

Jacob was referred to Manchester Children's Hospital, and on 13 July had his first appointment with Dr Ed Wraith, one of the leading experts on Hunter Syndrome and related genetic disorders. Many subsequent visits were made over the years: some involved Jacob being admitted for several days to undergo tests and others simply for periodical check-ups. When he was an in-patient, Mary and Andy stayed in family accommodation near the hospital. They always spoke highly of the hospital but, bearing in mind that at that stage of his life, Jacob was not as 'ill' as some of the other children, the environment they were in, with many very sick and terminally ill children, was a sad one. One of these was a little girl who was very ill with a genetic disorder, with whose mother Andy and Mary became friendly. Her daughter, who was about two years old, was terribly deformed, blind, deaf and had to be fed through a tube. She was totally unaware of the world around her and did not acknowledge her parents. Despite this, Andy told me, the mother said she didn't know how he and Mary could cope, knowing that they would lose Jacob at a young age. Several months later, Andy was contacted by Manchester police and asked questions about the mother of that little girl who had evidently died, they suspected, as a result of her life-support tubes being disconnected. Andy was unable to assist the police and I do not know the outcome of their investigations.

On 23 July 1995, Jacob returned to Manchester Children's Hospital to have his tonsils and adenoids removed and to have grommets inserted to improve his hearing. This was the first of several operations and procedures Jacob had to endure. Andy told us of the trauma of having to help restrain Jacob in order that the anaesthetic mask could be put on him. The operation certainly did improve his breathing though.

During his life, Jacob was a patient at various hospitals but his condition was monitored throughout by Dr Wraith at Manchester. He had several grommet operations to improve his hearing and these were usually done at Brighton by the consultant, Mr Harries. There is obviously a risk involved with any operation but with Jacob the risk was even greater. Because of the condition of his heart, anaesthetizing him was cause for concern and eventually Andy and Mary were told that no more operations would be possible, regardless of the complication, as the risk was too high. One of the symptoms of Hunter Syndrome is that the patient's Achilles tendons tighten up, causing them eventually to walk completely on tiptoes. Sometimes it is possible to operate to relieve the tension but that was not possible with Jacob. For most of his life he walked on his toes, unable to put his feet flat on the floor. We never knew if he was in pain, he rarely showed it - his pain barrier seemed remarkably high.

By the age of about eight, Jacob's breathing became much more laboured, he had a rasping cough and he often choked when eating. It was harrowing to witness, and on many occasions Mary or Andy would have to take food from Jacob's mouth and throat to stop him choking. About two weeks before his death, Anne and I were having tea with Mary and the boys when Jacob started to choke on his food. His face began to turn blue and Mary carried out the Heimlich manoeuvre in order to prevent him choking to death. Anne and I found it very frightening but Mary and Andy were used to dealing with such situations and never panicked.

Although Mary and Andy generally felt the NHS offered very good treatment for Jacob, particularly from such people as Dr Wraith and Mr Harries, there were times when they felt let down and frustrated. On several occasions, when Jacob had been choking or his breathing was particularly bad, he would have to be taken to hospital. One particular time, at Worthing Hospital, Jacob was examined by a doctor who, noting that his breathing was very laboured., looked in his mouth and then said that she thought his problem was his enlarged tonsils – Mary politely informed the doctor that Jacob's tonsils had been removed many months previously! I know this happened because I was there at the time, and while I appreciate that we all make mistakes – whatever our walk of life – when your child is seriously ill this sort of thing does not exactly inspire confidence.

It was a somewhat surreal situation in the early months after diagnosis in that Jacob, apart from his regular coughs, appeared to be like any other two-year-old and it was difficult to accept that he had a terminal illness. I spent many hours in the library and on the internet, looking at websites in order to glean as much information as possible about Hunter Syndrome. Mary was quite remarkable in her research, so much so that on one visit to Worthing Hospital a doctor told Mary that she was far more of an expert on MPS than he was.

The first sign that Jacob was different from other children of his age was his prominent forehead and lack of speech development. Prior to his diagnosis, Mary, Andy and any visitors would keep any noise in the house to a minimum when Jacob was sleeping, not knowing that his hearing was very poor. He gradually developed the typical features of a 'Hunter boy', which made him look unlike a normal child. We had to accept the fact that he would be stared at and there were several times when that happened and children showed how unknowingly cruel they can be. Jacob loved nothing more than watching other boys and girls playing, he was unaware that he was different and he certainly didn't understand if he was being talked about. Mary took him swimming on one occasion and two young boys pointed at Jacob and made comments about his looks. She went home in tears but realized that it was something she was going to have to face and accept.

From the time Jacob was diagnosed, Andy was not required to carry out his normal SAS duties, he was more or less on permanent compassionate leave. They continued to pay him and allowed the family to stay in their accommodation for about a year, until Andy was finally discharged in 1996. He realized that he would have to leave the army in order to devote more time to Jacob. He has never once complained about having to make that decision but sacrificing his army career must have been hard for him, he was so proud to have served in the SAS. In hindsight, I think it's a pity that Andy did not remain in the army, if not the SAS, in a position that would allow him more time at home to assist with Jacob. I am sure he would have progressed and been promoted and, hopefully, the army could have given the family the much-needed support in coping with Jacob's needs.

After Andy's discharge from the army, he and Mary moved to Worthing, where they bought a small house not far from both sets of parents. They knew that from then on their whole life would be dictated by Jacob's condition but we were determined to help them in whatever way we could, even if it was only by providing moral support. They were now surrounded by the love of family and friends – and hopefully the future would be easier to face.

The circumstances certainly brought our family closer together. Shortly after Andy moved back to Worthing, Steve came over from America to visit and, together with Chris, they went on a 'pub crawl'. Steve later told me that in addition to drinking a lot they talked a great deal about Jacob and the future. Andy found it hard to accept that he was eventually going to see his first-born child die. Steve also said that since that night, when the three boys shared their sorrow, they had never felt such love for one another, they had never been so close. That bond still exists today, despite some very difficult times we have all been through.

Andy and Mary, I know, having accepted Jacob's prognosis, considered their future, either with or without other children. It was a very difficult decision to make and when one thinks of the consequences of it one realizes their dilemma. Both of them obviously loved children, and the thought of going through life without another child, once Jacob had died, would be heartbreaking. On the other hand, if they decided that for Jacob to share his remaining years with a brother or sister would be wonderful for him, what effect would his eventual death have on the sibling? Andy and Mary also knew that as Mary was a carrier of the MPS gene there was a one in four chance of a male offspring inheriting the syndrome, whereas there was no risk for a female.

After moving to Worthing, they subsequently decided that they would have another baby, and when Mary became pregnant in the summer of 1997 everyone was delighted. However, we knew that if the baby was a boy and Hunter Syndrome was diagnosed, Andy and Mary would once more have to face the dreadful situation that they had experienced with Henry.

Early in the pregnancy a scan showed that the baby was a boy and an amniocentesis was performed on Mary to test for MPS. One can only guess at the thoughts that went through Andy's and Mary's minds as they awaited the test result. Anne and I certainly had subdued thoughts and emotions – until we heard the outcome that the boy Mary was carrying was a healthy baby. Words cannot describe how happy and relieved everyone was for Andy and Mary. Jacob was to have a little brother who they would see grow up and, hopefully, achieve everything in life that, sadly, Jacob would not.

The months seemed to go by very quickly and on 26 February 1998, Mary gave birth to a healthy baby, George, at Worthing Hospital. Shortly after his birth George was introduced to his big brother, who presented him with his first present, a cuddly toy. Jacob was so happy sitting on the bed and, with a little help from Mum, holding George tightly. Mary and George went home a day or two after the birth and Jacob just couldn't wait to show him his toys. Andy and Mary had to keep a close watch on Jacob though, as he tended to be quite boisterous and didn't know his own strength. He was touchingly happy helping Mary with George, fetching and carrying and doing little odd jobs for her. As George grew older the boys loved having baths together and, until Jacob became more ill, they liked nothing more than playing together in the garden. They had their tantrums, as all boys do when they take each other's toys, but they always seemed to enjoy each other's company. Jacob did not show any jealousy towards George, and we all made a special effort to share our love and attention between both boys. This was particularly important where George was concerned because Jacob's needs were greater.

By the time George was about four, he understood that Jacob was poorly and needed a lot of help and attention, but he seemed to be remarkably tolerant of the situation. I do not know if he was told, or understood, that his brother would die, but there is no doubt that George played a big part in making Jacob's life a happy one. I am sure Jacob appreciated having a younger brother and George can be proud of bringing that extra bit of happiness into his life.

Chapter 3
The Happy Years

Because we knew from a very early stage that Jacob had a terminal illness and would probably not live into his teenage years, Andy and Mary were determined that he should lead as normal a life as possible and for as long as his slowly deteriorating condition would allow. It was impressed on them by Jacob's consultant that the longer they were able to stimulate his brain, the longer would be the period until he eventually regressed. That certainly proved to be the case and Mary, particularly, worked very hard to ensure that happened. However, in those early years, family life was not dictated by Jacob's illness, and visits to the shops, restaurants and the park were the norm, as with any young family.

Although his speech was never the same as a normal boy of his age, up until about the last two years of his life, when Jacob had very little discernible speech, he had a reasonable vocabulary and it was always possible to understand him and his needs. He would talk in what can best be described as 'pidgin English'. Being quite deaf, he wore a hearing aid but his parents learned a little basic sign language, which they taught him, not to the extent of having a conversation or constructing sentences, but using signs to indicate his needs, such as signalling for a drink or food. When he was happy and he felt OK, Jacob would give the 'thumbs-up' sign.

Many things remind me of my little grandson and bring a smile to my face. His hearing aid is one such, when I recall the occasion when, with Mary out of the kitchen, Jacob put his hearing aid in the microwave – which promptly blew up and caught fire! Jacob was not really able to fully understand the difference between right and wrong. It was not possible to sit down and reason with him as one would with a normal child of a similar age. He was sometimes naughty, like any little boy, but often did not quite understand why what he had done was unacceptable..He would at times kick out at anyone near him, including his little brother. Charlie, Jacob's dog, which he loved dearly, quickly learned to move out of the way when Jacob was in one of those moods.

For the first four or five years of his life, Jacob was able to walk and run more or less normally and he became very strong physically. However, he did get tired fairly quickly and when his condition caused him permanently to walk on tiptoes, he would spend time in his wheelchair or pushchair, content to watch other people enjoying themselves. Jacob always seemed happy though. He absolutely loved watching everyone having a good time, and as a result we all have many wonderful memories of times spent enjoying life with Jacob.

One time I always remember fondly was when Anne and I spent a few days staying with Andy and Mary in Hereford. While Anne and Mary went shopping, Andy and I took Jacob to the local park, and after playing on the swings and slide we went to the nearby river to feed the ducks. Jacob sat in his pushchair and watched as his dad showed him how to throw the bread he had brought with us to the ever-increasing number of ducks that were gathering, but Jacob had other ideas. He suddenly jumped out of his pushchair and started to run down the riverbank towards the water shouting 'Bread! Bread!' Andy ran after him and caught him just before he reached the shallow water. Jacob was not at all happy that his feathered friends should have the stale bread and he insisted that he should eat some. He always had a good appetite; we often commented that he could 'eat for England'!

Jacob attended three schools in Worthing that catered for children with special needs and disabilities and they do a wonderful job. He particularly liked going to The Camelia Botnar Centre and, later, to Highdown School. He participated in all the class activities – colouring, painting, listening to stories and the like – although he was never able to read or write. Mary told us that when he was at Highdown, although Jacob was allocated to a particular class, on some days he himself would decide which class he wanted to go in. He would wander out of his own classroom into another and just sit down and watch the other children. The staff were very tolerant and allowed Jacob to do it because it made him happy, and that was a far better choice than forcing him to do something. Several stories involving Jacob at school still make us laugh.

Like most schools, Jacob's presented a nativity play at Christmastime, to which parents and friends were invited. All children were involved in some way, including the severely disabled in wheelchairs. One year, Jacob was cast as the innkeeper and his role was to sit outside his inn holding a large beer glass – to quote Andy, 'Like father like son!' – and wait for Joseph and Mary to ask for a room. Jacob had the whole audience in fits of laughter because from the very beginning, and more or less throughout the play, he kept jumping up and shouting 'No room! No room!' One of the teachers tried to tell the budding young thespian that he had to wait for his cue but Jacob had obviously learned his lines well and wanted a starring role.

We also attended the annual Harvest Thanksgiving at the school. Each child was asked to bring an item of food, and they sat on the stage holding whatever they had brought, which would in due course be placed on a table, blessed by the priest and subsequently distributed to local elderly folk. Jacob had brought a loaf of sliced bread as his gift and he sat on the stage proudly holding it as the short service of thanksgiving started. After a couple of minutes, our grandson opened his loaf and started to eat it. Not content with that, he began shouting out 'Butter! Butter!' He was allowed to eat one slice of bread, minus butter, and persuaded to leave the rest. As I said earlier, Jacob could eat for England.

Throughout his life Jacob loved watching videos. His favourite characters were Barney, Mickey Mouse and the killer whale Willy. In fact it was Barney's song, 'I love you, you love me' that was played at the service held prior to Jacob's funeral. His real favourite, though, was Willy, which he adored, particularly after going on holiday to Florida and seeing the whale in action. While there he was taken swimming with dolphins and although a little wary at first – he tried to punch one on the nose – he did enjoy it and some beautiful photographs were taken. Jacob's love of Willy even produced a lighter moment during Andy's trial. After several witnesses testified that Jacob enjoyed nothing more than watching the *Free Willy* video, the Judge commented to the effect that 'We can assume that had Jacob gone on *Mastermind* he would have been somewhat of an expert on *Free Willy*.'

Our beloved grandson used to visit us and sit and watch the *Free Willy* video while holding a toy replica of the whale. At the point in the film where Willy swims and jumps to freedom in the ocean, Jacob always became very excited, waved his arms about and shouted "Free Willy! Free Willy!' When I close my eyes I can hear him now and we still have his little toy whale to remind us of the pleasure he gave us.

Jacob's love of anything to do with Mickey Mouse stemmed from his visit to America, to Disneyland, before George was born, which was arranged by his Uncle Steve, whom he called 'Uncle Weevie'. Steve worked with several airlines in America, and Delta Airlines kindly funded the trip to Florida for Jacob and his parents. They rented a holiday home in Orlando and Jacob loved jumping in the swimming pool with his cousins, Noel and Chelsea.

Andy and Mary later took Jacob and George to Disneyland, Paris, which they both enjoyed, especially George, but Jacob by that time was tiring very easily. A day trip to Lapland to visit Father Christmas was another memorable outing. However, while George loved it, Jacob's health was deteriorating by then, so he wasn't able to enjoy it quite as much.

Another holiday they really enjoyed was a visit, with Chris, to Cornwall. While there, they visited Anne's brother, Ray, and his family. Ray was at that time serving in the Fleet Air Arm and he took Jacob to look over a helicopter. He remembered that for a long time afterwards and whenever he saw a photo of Ray he would say 'Helicopter, helicopter.'

After returning from his various holidays and trips Jacob would delight in showing us his photographs, proudly pointing out pictures of him with Mickey Mouse and various other characters and friends. When he came to visit us he would sit for ages looking through photo albums. Anne rearranged the photographs in all of our many albums so that whichever one Jacob looked at he would always recognize the family, friends and places he'd visited. He would point at the photograph and excitedly say the name of the person he knew.

Jacob spent a great deal of time watching television and as a result had his favourite characters. Among them were Dale Winton and *Supermarket Sweep,* the Chuckle Brothers, whose picture he had on his bedroom wall, and local television personality and children's entertainer Dave Benson, who I believe kindly visited Jacob at home on one occasion.

After moving to Worthing from Hereford, although Andy and Mary were separated for a period, and Andy also spent time away from home when working for a video rental business, Anne and I did see quite a lot of Jacob. During the years before he became really poorly we took him for trips out, usually with Mary, sometimes with Andy, if he was home.

We have happy memories of days on Worthing beach, pub lunches and visiting various relatives. Jacob had a remarkable long-term memory but a poor short-term one. In the years before his health deteriorated too far, the family would go out to lunch at various pub-restaurants. I remember being in the car with him and he would shout and point at some establishment he had been taken to several weeks before. But if you asked him what he had had for lunch that day, he could not remember.

Jacob's favourite outing was, I think, going to the Worthing Aquarena indoor swimming pool. He had no fear of water and he used to laugh and shout as he jumped into the water and I caught him.

We also made several visits with Mary and Jacob to Fishers Farm, where the children can see the animals up close, feed and stroke some of them. On one such visit Steve and his family were over from America and Jacob had great fun with his cousin, Noel. Although only a little older than Jacob, Noel was very good with him. He knew that Jacob was not as fit as he was but he understood and they had a fun day. We took a photograph of the boys sitting on the steps of an old horse-drawn caravan and several years later when Noel and his family were again visiting from America we replicated the photo. It is interesting but poignant to compare the two. Noel and Jacob were about the same age but the difference in their development is sadly obvious from the second photo.

Over the years we spent several very happy Christmases with Andy, Mary, Jacob and George. When Jacob was very young he adored Christmas, just like any little boy, and we have some lovely photographs of him with Father Christmas at the hospital where Anne was working. Mary would not give the boys all their presents on Christmas Day – just the main ones. She would keep some back and give them out over the next few days – Jacob loved this and I thought it was a great idea. During the last few years of his life, choosing Christmas and birthday presents for Jacob was a problem for us. At a fairly early age he started to lose interest in toys and as he got older, when given a present Jacob would love to rip the paper off and then show little interest in the contents, sometimes even throwing them away. He was happy to watch George playing with his toys and was not jealous of him in the least. Jacob did love his videos, though, also books and clothes: he liked nothing better than trying on new clothes – especially if it was a Chelsea football kit.

In 2002 Steve and his family spent Christmas with us and, together with Mary, Jacob, George and Mary's mum, Gwen, we went to see a pantomime, *Puss in Boots.* Jacob seemed to like it but by that time he wasn't able to concentrate for too long, so he didn't see it all the way through, and Mary had to take him out and occupy him until we joined them at the end of the show.

The last time we went out with Mary, Jacob and George was on Father's Day 2004, when Andy was in Iraq. We booked a meal at a local pub but because there was no room for us inside we sat in the garden under a large marquee. Jacob was in his wheelchair and was quite happy watching George running about and playing with other children. Just as we started our meal the heavens opened and there was a huge thunderstorm. Everyone ran for cover in the pub – except us! We decided to stay put. The problem was that the marquee started to leak and before long we all began to get wet. Jacob and George thought it was absolutely hilarious. It was a very hot day and George seemed to delight in getting as wet as possible. We all laughed and when Mary, Anne and I started a chorus of *Singin' in the Rain,* Jacob laughed even more. He was so happy. Because of the wet state we were all in I phoned Tina and asked her to bring us some towels and dry clothing for the boys. I will always remember that Father's Day, everyone was so happy.

The one abiding memory Anne and I have of Jacob is his insistence that everyone should be 'happy'. From an early age, and even more so as he grew older, Jacob more or less demanded that of everyone. I vividly remember going to visit him and knocking on the door. He would run down the hallway on his tiptoes, open the door and throw his arms around Anne and me. He would then round up everyone in the house, Andy, Mary, George whoever was there, get them to stand in a circle and then all kiss each other. Jacob would then shout, 'Big hugs, big hugs! Happy Nannie, happy Grandad, happy Mummy, happy Daddy, happy George and happy Jacob.'

Mary told me that when she took the boys out it was a little embarrassing at times because if she met someone she knew maybe not so well Jacob would still insist on 'Big hugs!'

Yes, our wonderful grandson certainly knew how to do HAPPY! I like to think that, despite all we have been through, we can continue to follow the example he set.

During these times fundraising played a part in all our lives and one one memorable spring day Anne sat on the bridge looking down at the murky waters of the river Arun, fifteen feet below. Should she jump or not? She was petrified but knew she had to do it for Jacob. She had only gone along to Littlehampton to support others in a fundraising event but there she was, dressed in a tight wetsuit, about to do something the likes of which she had never done before. Anne herself admits that she could not be described as an 'action woman' but, very bravely, she jumped. She was immediately picked up by the waiting rescue boat and adjourned with the rest of the brave souls to a nearby pub for a well-deserved drink. I am so proud of Anne for pushing herself to do that jump. Mary also jumped, as did Jacob's cousin Rebecca and his uncle Terry who organized the event to raise money for the MPS Society.

Naturally, we all wanted to do anything we could to help the MPS Society, the charity that deals directly with families who have children suffering with Hunter Syndrome. On learning of Jacob's prognosis we all felt so helpless. None of us had ever heard of mucopolysaccharidosis and the more we read and researched it the more impotent we felt. Andy and Mary contacted the MPS Society, whose founder and Chief Executive is Christine Lavery, MBE, a wonderful lady who had lost her own son to Hunter Syndrome several years previously. Christine was always very kind, knowledgeable and supportive to all the family, and has become a good friend.

It was obvious from an early stage that Jacob and his parents would require respite care, which was provided initially by Naomi House Children's Hospice near Winchester and later at Chestnut Tree House Hospice, a brand-new facility that was to be built in Worthing. The Children's Hospice Movement provides vitally needed support for terminally ill children and relies on fundraising and donations. They receive very little government funding. The MPS Society receives none at all.

During the first few years of his life Jacob spent many happy times at Naomi House Hospice, Winchester, which was the nearest to his home in Worthing. At that time Sussex had no hospice provision. I have so much admiration for the staff who work in hospices such as Naomi House: their love and dedication is wonderful, and the respite they provide for families with children who have a terminal illness is fantastic. I went with Andy to collect Jacob after one of his stays and saw at first hand the work that is done to care for children with various conditions, some of whom require one-to-one nursing twenty-four hours a day. The facilities included a light room and a swimming pool, and the children who are able are taken on trips out.

Although Jacob's condition was terminal, on his visits to Naomi House, particularly in the early days, he was one of the more active children. He had his own room with television and video, and was able to roam freely about the place, play in the gardens and kick a football about. He was always on tiptoes though, and tired very easily. He would then go and lie on his bed, watch his videos and drop off to sleep. The nursing he – and all the children – received was one-to-one. The staff loved him and encouraged him to help with small chores. There was nothing he loved more than helping to lay the table at meal times, or going from room to room watching what the other children were doing. Jacob would stay at Naomi House for up to a week and although he was always pleased to see Andy and Mary when they collected him, he rarely cried when they left him. In fact Jacob very rarely cried at all. He would do so if he hurt himself but although he was probably in constant pain, especially towards the end of his life, he did not show it. Jacob always loved going to Naomi House, he was happy there.

Anne and I recall Jacob telling us about one stay he had at the hospice when he was taken out on two trips. He explained that he and his friends had been taken for a ride in the car that had been used in the film *Chitty Chitty, Bang Bang*. He also said that he had been 'motor racing' and driving racing cars! It transpired that he had been taken to a local motor-racing circuit and watched cars speeding round the track – he evidently loved it.

In 2002 land just outside Worthing was donated and a fundraising campaign was launched to raise approximately £5,000,000 to build the Chestnut Tree House Hospice. Jacob was selected to be one of the children to promote the campaign, and a lovely photo of him wearing his Chelsea football kit appeared on the front of thousands of brochures.

Many of our friends and family joined us in various fundraising activities for the Chestnut Tree House building fund, and these included sponsored walks, horseracing evenings and raffles. Our friends Paul and Brenda Murray, who were fantastically supportive during the difficult times, organized several fundraising evenings at their house, one of which was a wine tasting – I can't think why, but none of us remember much about that night . . . Although we were all very much aware of the reasons for being involved in these activities, in the early years it was difficult to relate any of it to Jacob's condition. He was active and life for him was fun, his deterioration was a slow process.

Our son, Chris, who was at the time a producer with Sky Sport, organized a charity football match at Brentford Football Club in which he and Andy played, along with many well-known professional footballers and ex-England players. Another event was a go-karting day, where Jacob was absolutely delighted to see his dad driving like a lunatic. I loved watching Jacob laughing and having fun. He was a boisterous, fun-loving child with an infectious giggle, but beneath all that there was this knowledge, this awful awareness that day-by-day he was becoming more and more ill. I always found that the most painful thing.

The driving force behind the fundraising was a wonderful lady, Lesley-Anne Lloyd, whom we got to know very well. During several discussions with Lesley-Anne she gave me an interesting insight into the world of fundraising, particularly where it involves a hospice.

Chestnut Tree House was built specifically to cater for children, mainly in the Sussex area, who have a terminal illness, and to provide respite for their families. The building can cater for up to ten children at any one time and approximately £2,000,000-plus per annum is required to keep it operating (the small government grant is around £200,000 p.a.). The fundraising publicity produced great response, particularly from the local community. It is amazing how generous folk can be. I know of one person who knew of Jacob's prognosis and, on hearing about the Chestnut Tree Appeal, donated £20,000. However, a very small minority of the public evidently objected, particularly about whether any money from public funds should be used to build a hospice.

Basically, they argue, why spend a vast sum of money funding something that will only benefit a small number of patients with terminal illnesses, when the money could be better spent on saving the lives of those with life-threatening conditions who will die if they do not receive urgent treatment? This poses a very difficult moral dilemma and, while I respect all opinions, I can only say that Jacob's experiences in respite care were invaluable for him and his parents. The support and help they received was boundless.

In 2003, Chestnut Tree House Hospice was opened by HRH Princess Alexandra. Jacob attended the ceremony and his brother George presented a bouquet of flowers to the Princess. Like all children's hospices Chestnut Tree House does a magnificent job in a very difficult and demanding area, particularly in the final days of the lives of terminally ill children. From its opening, great support was given to Jacob and his parents until the time of his death.

However, I do have some criticism which is intended to be constructive, in the lack of support given to Anne and me following Jacob's death.

The Worthing Hospice state in their literature that they provide counselling at the time of bereavement for all the family including grandparents and under normal circumstances I am sure they do. However after Jacob's death , although requesting counselling Andy, Anne and I received none. I believe Mary did. I do understand the reasons for this but I feel the situation could have been handled better. I have since had meetings with staff from Chestnut Tree House in order that we can all learn from the experience and let us hope that, in the unlikely event of similar circumstances occurring it would be handled differently.

Prior to Jacob's funeral a service to commemorate his life was held at Chestnut Tree House. Very soon after that it was evident that some staff at the Hospice were interviewed by Police and might be called as witnesses for the prosecution. They were instructed for legal reasons not to talk any of us.

Despite several calls requesting counselling for Anne and me our calls were ignored and no contact was made with us. Under the circumstances I feel someone at the Hospice could have passed our request to another Hospice or organisation that had had no dealings with Jacob, were not involved with any legal proceedings and might have given us the help we required.

Anne and I supported each other throughout that terrible time and, although being offered counselling much later, we declined it. By that time we were at peace with the knowledge and acceptance that Jacob was free from his suffering.

Chapter 4
A Marriage under Pressure

There is no doubt that Andy and Mary's marriage could not be described as 'one made in heaven'. They are two very strong-minded, volatile people and from the outset it was obvious that to have a lasting relationship they would both have to respect one another's opinion. During their marriage they did separate on several occasions, sometimes due to Andy taking work away from home after leaving the army and sometimes because they felt they just could not live together. During those times Andy would always see Jacob and George, although at one point his relationship with Mary was so strained that he had to obtain an access order from court to enable him to do so. Despite this, both parents made several attempts to make the marriage work and get back together.

Marriages break down for many reasons but it is a sad fact that in families where there is a disabled child, it is far from unusual for one or other of the parents to leave, as they find it impossible to cope with the stress. Andy and Mary had to deal with Jacob's deteriorating condition knowing that he would eventually die; Andy had to leave the army, which had offered him a good future; Mary had to cope with an ongoing medical problem, a kidney disease, which involved her being admitted to hospital several times; they had to move house and have their new home renovated in order to accommodate Jacob's needs. It is hardly surprising that they constantly felt under pressure.

They had the frequent hospital visits with Jacob in addition to the times he was admitted in an emergency. Mary had many battles with the social services and local authorities throughout Jacob's life, fighting to get such basic things as nappies, let alone special shoes and schooling for him. Both she and Andy attended a number of conferences with social workers, doctors and other healthcare professionals but after several, in Andy's view, fruitless meetings, he stopped going. He became very frustrated with the social services and got quite angry with them, mainly for what he believed to be their lack of action or failure to follow through with recommendations. This was highlighted when Jacob was assessed for a special needs boarding school about a year before his death. Mary told us that the school was in Surrey and he was accepted – however the funding for him to attend was to be provided by the local West Sussex authority and, due to lack of funds, they had to refuse the request and the school placement was taken by a child from another county.

Despite Jacob's constant and ever-increasing needs, Andy and Mary did their best to ensure that George's needs were never neglected and we all made a point of giving as much love to him as to his brother. From an early age, George was told that Jacob was different from him and George often used to say to Anne and me 'Jacob is poorly, you know.' When George was small, Jacob was his 'big brother' and in those days he was able to run around and play football. He was strong and had a very powerful kick, as George often found out when he was on the receiving end of one. In the early days, Jacob could outrun George and he would chase him around the garden and push him over. As George grew up though, it was not long before he could easily outrun Jacob, who would chase him for a short distance but then give up. Eventually he just wouldn't bother, which we found rather sad, as it was a further sign that Jacob's health was deteriorating.

In 1995, not long after Jacob was diagnosed Andy and Mary came to stay with us for a few days. Anne and I babysat while Jacob's parents went out for a meal. On returning they went to bed, Andy sleeping in a room with Jacob and Mary in the spare room. At about four o'clock in the morning the phone rang. It was Gwen, Mary's mother, to tell us that Mary had been admitted to Worthing Hospital suffering from tablet overdose. She had apparently taken a large amount of pills of some kind and then walked from our house to the hospital. No one had heard her get up and leave – we were dumbfounded. Andy went immediately to see her and we looked after Jacob. Mary asked Andy to bring Jacob to the hospital to see her but he refused -he was angry with her for what looked like an attempt at suicide. He viewed it as a selfish act with no thought for him or Jacob. She was kept in hospital for a few hours under observation and then discharged. Was it a selfish act by Mary or was it a cry for help ?

When Andy and Mary moved from Hereford back to Worthing in the summer of 1996 we obviously saw a lot more of them and the children. We often babysat for them. When Andy was away, working for a video company, we knew Mary had her hands full and frequently asked her to just shout if she needed any help – perhaps taking George for a couple of hours or picking him up from school or maybe shopping – but she very rarely did. I know that Mary's mother Gwen did help a lot and always gave her great support.

Mary is a very proud and independent person. She is a good mother and I admire her for that. Andy has described himself as 'a good father but a lousy husband' and that is probably somewhere near the truth. I don't think it's right to be judgemental about someone else's marriage; there are only ever two people who know what goes on in a partnership. However, Anne and I both feel that had they asked for more help both from within and perhaps outside the family, life could have been a little easier for them.

After they moved to Worthing in 1996 the marriage did seem to settle down a bit. Andy, after working for a video company, set up his own video rental shop in Worthing, Jacob was attending school, which he liked, and George was born in 1998. Andy and Mary's relationship appeared stable, although, like most couples, they had their arguments. As regards his illness, these were probably Jacob's best years and his parents did their best to enjoy them with him.

There is no doubt that both Andy and Mary drank too much at times, which is probably hardly surprising. In addition, Mary was taking drugs for a chronic medical condition. This always concerned Andy, who, although like most people of his age admits to trying cannabis on the odd occasion in the past, says he is very much against hard drugs. His view was that Mary was being prescribed drugs for her kidney complaint and unwisely mixing them with alcohol.

Andy and Mary stayed together for five years but tension between them built up and eventually, in 2000, Andy left home and rented a flat nearby. They lived apart until 2002 but Andy did see the boys when Mary agreed to it. During that period, Anne and I became very worried about Mary's health, both physical and mental, and when we visited the house there were various signs that gave us cause for concern. I talked things over with Andy and trusted members of the family – I knew I could not speak to Mary, but felt I couldn't let things go on as they were, so I did two things which I felt were right at the time.

Firstly, I phoned the family's social worker to express my concern.

I was told not to worry and that 'If you think that family is cause for concern, you should see some of the other cases we have to deal with.' No doubt that is true but I did not find those comments helpful. Secondly, I went to see Mary's family doctor. Quite naturally, she would not discuss anything whatsoever to do with Mary or the family but she did thank me for going to see her and alerting her to my worries.

Perhaps I could be criticized for taking such action but at the time I felt it was the right thing to do for both Mary and the boys. They were being perfectly well looked after but we were very worried about Mary's health and wanted to help her but didn't know how. I felt it far better to have reported our concerns rather than to have done nothing.

Andy later told me that he also had spoken to Mary's doctor of his concerns. He, Andy, knew that she was taking both prescribed and unprescribed drugs, but thankfully, Mary's general condition did gradually improve. However, she was constantly under the strain of coping with Jacob's needs, looking after George and not knowing if her marriage was going to last.

As time went on, Jacob's condition deteriorated and he became more difficult to handle. He was strong and if he didn't want to do something, he would either do it in his own time or not at all. They would go out shopping, and he would suddenly decide to lie on the floor shouting and become a 'dead weight'. He was heavy and it was sometimes impossible to pick him up. If Andy was there he could lift him but for Mary, particularly if George was there as well, it was difficult. Jacob would at times kick out at anybody who was close to him for no apparent reason. Sometimes Jacob would refuse to get out of the car and no amount of coaxing would persuade him to do so. It was just a matter of waiting, at times for quite a few minutes, until he decided to get out. Towards the end of his life, when it was necessary for him to wear nappies again, he would suddenly take all his clothes off and throw his nappies around the room, changing his clothes several times a day. He could not be reasoned with and one had to accept his mood swings and just go along with them. It seemed to us, as Jacob regressed and his behaviour changed, that it was probably as a result of his frustration.

We saw all this on a number of occasions but Mary had to deal with it on a daily basis, often without Andy's support.

One thing Jacob has taught me is to try not to prejudge any situation. We all do it to a certain extent. How many times have you been in a supermarket and heard a child screaming and shouting, with its mother sometimes threatening it – often ignoring it? In the past, like most people, I would have thought, Why doesn't that woman keep that child under control? He/she needs to be taught how to behave! I was probably right most times but now I am more tolerant and wonder if perhaps there is some underlying factor causing the child to behave in such a disruptive manner.

Another incident Mary related to us also highlighted this. When Jacob attended his special school he would be picked up each day by taxi; he was usually excited, both at going to school and also at seeing one of his school friends who was also in the car, and on one such journey, he started to kick the back of the driver's seat. The driver told him to stop, and when he didn't, the man told him that he was going to tell his mother that he was a naughty boy and a baby and he would have to wear nappies (which he did not have to do at that time). I am not sure if Jacob knew exactly what the driver had said but the other child did, and was so upset by it that when they got to school he told the teacher. I'm not criticizing the driver but it shows how easy it is for an adult to upset a child when they really have no intention of doing so. How many of us remember things that were said to us when we were young that we still remember as adults? I know I do.

When I think back to poor Jacob and his behaviour I remember that it was just not possible to reason with him when he was in what we came to call one of his 'No' moods.

As his illness worsened, Jacob's joints stiffened up and he had great difficulty climbing our stairs, in the end finding it virtually impossible. Anne recalls the sad regression in Jacob and one particular incident near the end of his life left a lasting impression. He always loved climbing the stairs when he visited us and he would stand at the top, looking at the family photographs we have on the walls. On this particular day, he decided that he wanted to go upstairs, and Anne stood at the bottom ready to follow behind. Jacob only managed to climb about three or four stairs but could get no further. He turned to his Nannie with a sad look on his face and that was the last time he attempted to climb our stairs. That upset Anne very much, so much so that we discussed the possibility of moving to a bungalow so that Jacob would be happier when visiting us. We actually viewed several but then events changed all our futures. Having anticipated such deterioration and planned for it, Andy,

Mary, Jacob and George had already moved to a very nice bungalow in Worthing. It had a large garden and the boys had their own rooms. While he was living there Andy did a good deal of decorating and made some DIY improvements.

Andy has been criticized for walking out of the family home for two years, leaving Mary to cope with Jacob and George. I do not pretend to know if Andy's decision to leave his family for the time he did was right or wrong. Anne felt that, because of Jacob's condition and the difficulty of coping with his increasing strength, Andy had no choice but to stay, no matter what. I tended to agree with her at the time, but since then, and with the benefit of hindsight, I think I understand why he left.

Andy has told us that if at that time his relationship with Mary had been a normal, loving one, he could have coped with Jacob's condition. But it was not. He accepts that the pressures on the marriage due to Jacob's illness were tremendous both physically and mentally, but that both he and Mary were to blame for the breakdown. He admitted at his subsequent trial that he can be selfish at times and he said he thought Mary could be stubborn and irrational at times. They rarely argued vehemently in front of Anne and me, but Andy has told us that they did when we weren't there – and at times it would really upset the boys.

Ultimately, Andy felt that the situation, apart from making him and Mary very unhappy, was likely to affect Jacob and, especially, George. He believed that, provided he was still able to see the boys and give Mary the support she needed, then it was better to leave the matrimonial home. Unfortunately, for various reasons, Andy was not always able to give that support.

I have been lucky in that I have had a long stable marriage, but like many people, I have seen marriages break up, some involving young children, some older and some grown-up. Many people are of the opinion that if small children are involved in a bad marriage, then the parents should stay together for the sake of those children, no matter what. I believe that, provided the parties can agree on sensible access to their children, then separation is probably a better scenario than allowing the children to grow up seeing and believing that warring parents is the norm. I have seen some parents who have separated when the children were much older, where the separation has probably affected the children more as they are able to think, analyse and judge the situation as they see it, often taking sides with one or other parent. Small children, on the other hand, are very resilient and will accept a situation for what it is, without much analysis or judgement. Provided they are not 'brainwashed' by one parent or the other and the parents are honest with them, then there is no reason why they should not have a happy upbringing.

Hopefully that will be George's future.

It is not for me, or anyone else, to judge Andy's decision to leave home, but he did it in what he thought was the best interests of his sons at the time and, eventually, after a period apart, it is great credit to both him and Mary that they did get back together and try to make their marriage work. Unfortunately Jacob's death changed their future.

On leaving the army, Andy worked for a video rental company and eventually set up his own business, opening a video shop in Worthing. He worked hard to make it a success for about two years but struggled financially. Although Andy was separated from Mary for a while, by January 2004 their relationship had improved and they were living together again. However, mainly due to increasing financial difficulties with his business, Andy decided to apply for the position of a security operative in Iraq, and Mary was in agreement.

He knew that the work he would be doing was extremely dangerous but the financial rewards were great. Following the invasion of Iraq there was a big demand for security staff, and Andy's training and experience in the SAS and Bosnia made him ideal for the post. He undertook a firearms course in Spain, followed by training in close protection, self-defence and driving skills, and on 24 April 2004 I took him to Heathrow and he left for Iraq.

While in Iraq, Andy was working in a four-man team with two vehicles. They were based in what is known as the 'Green Zone' and their job was to escort American bankers out of the 'Zone' to buildings in and around Baghdad. They also drove frequently to and from Baghdad airport, along what has been described as 'the most dangerous road in the world' due to the number of roadside bombs that were detonated.

Andy experienced a number of dangerous incidents during the three months he was there. One morning, his duty was to go down to a bridge and pick up Iraqi drivers. He did so and returned to the operations room, which was opposite the bridge. As he entered the room there was a huge explosion that blew all the windows out of the building, and everyone 'hit the floor'. It transpired that a suicide bomber had blown up the bridge, killing two Americans and several Iraqis. One of the injured was an Iraqi driver who was late arriving at the pick-up point. He suffered severe burns but survived.

In another incident, two of Andy's colleagues who were driving in a vehicle ahead of him were killed when their truck was blown up. Also, two of his close friends were shot, one in the shoulder and one in the head; thankfully both survived. After Andy had returned to the UK one of his team was killed, and he went to his funeral. Andy said that the bonding between the men was very good, all were ex-army personnel, they had to be or they wouldn't survive.

Sometimes, in order to reduce the risks of an ambush, they would dress as Iraqis but that, too, had its drawbacks. If they had a breakdown or a puncture and had to park up by the side of the road they could get into very deep trouble. It was a common ploy for bombers to pretend to change a flat tyre by the roadside and then attack British or American troops as they passed. Numerous American and British soldiers had been killed in this way and subsequently, if a vehicle was parked in an unusual place the Americans chose to shoot first and ask questions later and would shoot at any vehicle they thought looked suspicious.

Andy told me that once out of the Green Zone everyone was in immediate danger. Mortars were coming in constantly and virtually everyone had to be looked upon as a potential killer. He said it was a frightening experience but accepted it as part of the job.

During his time in Iraq Andy phoned Mary on most days and often spoke to George. Jacob was not able to talk to him, though, as by then his speech had gone.

On 9 July 2004, Andy came home on leave, fully intending to go back to Iraq. He was earning approximately £80,000 per annum, which sounds a lot but the risks were very high. He was promised that when he did go back he would be posted to a less risky area outside Baghdad.

Of course, not being in the military, on his return from Iraq Andy received no counselling or support. Was he suffering from post-traumatic stress disorder? What effect Andy's experiences in Bosnia and, particularly, Iraq had on him we will never know, but there is no doubt that various opinions of his mental state as a result of those experiences were discussed at great length later in court and had a bearing on the verdict.

When he got home Andy saw a huge change in Jacob – I think he was shocked at the deterioration that had taken place in just three months. Added to that were the pressures of dealing with several years of Jacob's illness, an unstable marriage and financial worries – a lot to cope with in anyone's life.

As I understand it, post-traumatic stress disorder – PTSD – is a subjective condition that can cause serious psychiatric and mental disorders and there are varying opinions within the medical profession as to exactly what it is and how it affects those suffering from it.

As a result of the wars in Iraq and Afghanistan, post-traumatic stress suffered by military personnel is now recognized, and those diagnosed receive counselling on their return from active service. During the First and Second World Wars, many military personnel were said to have suffered shell shock – something which today would most likely be diagnosed as PTSD. There is no doubt that some soldiers from those earlier wars did suffer severe psychological shock and the actions they subsequently took were wrongly interpreted, especially in the First World War , when some were executed for cowardice. There are many accounts of Vietnam veterans committing suicide or becoming alcoholics – again very likely as a result of PTSD. During and after those wars there was little if any counselling and many never recovered from their dreadful experiences. Andy told me that forces returning from war zones are offered counselling but that many decline because they feel they don't need it or they do not want their 'macho image' to be tarnished – not a wise view to take, but perhaps understandable.

Prior to Andy's trial he was interviewed by three psychiatrists, one of whom interviewed him twice. The first time was when he was in Lewes Prison, and its purpose was to assess the likelihood of Andy committing suicide and also his suitability to be granted bail. He was later assessed by two psychiatrists appointed by his defence team and again by the prosecution, so that they could give a professional opinion on Andy's state of mind when he ended Jacob's life, and especially to ascertain their views as to what brought about that state of mind.

Chapter 5
In Lewes Prison

On 28 July Andy made his first court appearance and was remanded in custody to Lewes Prison. Later that evening he phoned us. It was such a relief to hear his voice. It was the first time I had spoken to him since his arrest. He sounded quiet and didn't say much, other than that he was all right and that he wanted Mary to come to our house so that he could speak to her on the phone, as he was only able to call one registered number and all calls were monitored. Mary did subsequently speak to Andy from our home.

Prison visiting is very restricted and application to see a prisoner has to be made some days in advance. After several phone calls I managed to speak to the appropriate Prison Office and arranged three visits.

On Sunday 1 August, Chris, Steve who had come over from America and I visited Andy in Lewes Prison. During my police service I went into many prisons, although not Lewes, and I knew what to expect. Chris and Steve did not. There is a vast difference, though, between visiting a prisoner as a police officer on professional business and as a father visiting his son who is facing a charge of murdering his own son. Lewes is a Victorian prison built in 1853, it houses approximately 720 convicted and remand prisoners.

Since being remanded in custody, Andy had been in prison for four days before we saw him, and those four days seemed like a lifetime to Anne and me. We spoke to our son every day and he assured us that he was being treated well – but I knew that Andy would not want us to worry about his welfare and was only partially reassured. One hears so many stories of prisoners facing charges that involve children being assaulted and abused even while on remand, before they've been found guilty by a court . . . Although we probably all had such thoughts, however, we did not speak of them.

Steve, Chris and I entered the visitors' reception area of the prison, along with a number of others who were there to see inmates, some on remand awaiting trial and others who were serving a sentence. Several of the visitors had children with them, some very young. Andy had already told Mary and us that he did not want George to visit him in prison and I think it was the correct decision. Visitors are not allowed to take anything into the prison for prisoners, not even books or newspapers. We were searched and all our possessions were put in a locker. While this was being done, a prison warder asked my name and then told me that he felt very sorry for my son and that he believed he should not have been remanded to prison. Two other staff also said the same on different occasions. I must say that on our three visits we were treated with respect by all the staff with whom we came into contact.

We were taken to a very large room on the first floor, which was laid out with chairs on one side of a high desk and, together with the other visitors, we all sat down and waited. After a short time, the inmates started to enter the room and join their visitors. Steve, Chris and I stood up as we saw Andy approaching and I was determined not to show too much emotion. I leaned across the desk, put my arms around Andy and held him tightly. The boys did the same. I then saw a notice on the wall saying that no physical contact was to be made with the prisoners. We had just broken that rule, but so had every other visitor – the prison officers who were standing watching everyone did not seem to mind.

Like most of the other prisoners, Andy was wearing a prison-issue maroon T-shirt and jeans. He looked pale but otherwise seemed OK. Steve bought a cold drink and some chocolate from a machine, which Andy was pleased to have, and we started talking.

The boys and I had agreed beforehand that we'd let Andy do the talking – we didn't want to talk about Jacob's death if he didn't. Andy said little about what had happened to Jacob. All he said was he believed he had put an end to Jacob's suffering and that Jacob had 'asked him to end his life', he said he had seen it when he looked into Jacob's eyes. He said that he did not want Mary to be charged and that he was happy to accept responsibility for what had happened. He felt that if Mary were to be charged it would be devastating for George, he could even be placed in care. We all agreed.

Andy told us that his solicitor had visited him and that a psychiatrist had come to assess whether he might attempt suicide and to look at his suitability for bail.

Andy also told us what had happened to him since he'd been in

Lewes Prison. Very shortly after arriving by prison van from Chichester Court he was processed and given his prison number. He was seen by the Prison Governor, who told Andy that he had sympathy for him and also that he thought, under the circumstances, Andy should have been given bail rather than being committed to prison. He asked Andy if there was anything he wanted. Andy told the Governor that he did not wish to be placed in a cell with a drug addict or 'nutter'. Andy said that he knew drugs allegedly played a big part in prison life and he wanted nothing to do with that. He just wanted to 'keep his head down' and be given bail as soon as possible. Andy also said that, from the start, he knew that with his SAS training he would not have a problem handling his time in prison – no matter how long that might be.

He was placed in a cell with one other inmate, who I think had been in prison before and was back inside for burglary. His cellmate told Andy that he had been put with him in order to keep an eye on him and make sure he didn't attempt suicide. Andy thanked him and said he would wake him up and tell him when he was going to do it – typical of Andy's humour!

From day one, publicity regarding Jacob's death was vast. It was the headline news in virtually every national newspaper and extensively covered on every television and radio news report. Andy said that before he got to Lewes Prison he was concerned as to how he would be treated by other prisoners; however, he soon realized that because of the publicity, all of them knew who he was and why he was there and some expressed their sympathy for him and wished him good luck. Andy said that there was only one incident, when he was queuing up for dinner and another prisoner pointed him out and made a comment to the effect that 'He is the one who murdered a child'. Immediately another prisoner stepped in and told the accuser to 'shut up and mind his own business'. He had no other problems.

We spent about forty minutes with Andy and on leaving he asked us to pass on his love to Mary and George if we had the chance. He also told us not to bring Anne into prison to see him and we all agreed to that. Steve, Chris and I all felt relieved after seeing Andy and we were happy to put Anne's mind at rest after the visit.

From the time Jacob's death had become public knowledge the publicity had been enormous, which we knew would be inevitable. Following Andy's remand in custody, the press appeared to be sympathetic towards him. Several newspapers printed pictures of him being led into a prison van, outside Chichester Court and in handcuffs. They commented that they considered it unnecessary for Andy to be refused bail and that to place him in handcuffs was a disgrace.

That Andy had not been granted bail was upsetting. However, we were quite confident that it would only be for a short time and that at his next court appearance, on 5 August, he would be released.

Chris, Steve and I next visited Andy on Tuesday, 3 August. After being searched, we joined other visitors and queued up on a flight of stairs, waiting to be admitted to the visiting room. As we were waiting, we looked back down the stairs and there, at the bottom, standing in line with the visitors, was Andy with a prison officer! He gave us a wave and smiled. Andy had apparently been collected from his cell and the officer had taken him into the yard for some fresh air prior to seeing us. They had ended up coming into the building via the visitors' entrance and joined our queue – Andy asked the officer if he could join our line on the way out!

The next day, Tina and I visited him. Tina was very pleased to see her brother, who seemed well and talked generally about his prison experiences with his usual sense of humour. He was, though, rather tense, which was hardly surprising as he was due to appear at Lewes Crown Court the next day. His solicitor had told him that although he was going to apply for Andy's release on bail, he should not expect it and he should be prepared for a further remand in custody. If the application failed then they could apply to a judge in chambers for bail., We told him we loved him, to be positive and we would see him at court the next day.

Mary had been arrested on the evening of 24 July, kept in police custody until late on Tuesday 27, and released without charge. Andy was arrested with Mary but when she was released, he was charged with Jacob's murder, appeared in court the next day and was remanded in custody to Lewes Prison. It was during her days in police custody that Mary seemed to turn against Andy and subsequently gave evidence for the prosecution.

One obvious answer as to why Mary did this is that Andy ended Jacob's life without her agreement or knowledge. That scenario is I believe, to say the least questionable, and the facts and interpretation of them point possibly to a more complex but understandable explanation.

On the night of Jacob's death, Mary and Andy were both arrested on suspicion of his murder and taken to separate police stations for questioning. Neither was able to speak to the other until several days later, when Mary had been released without charge and Andy was on remand in Lewes Prison. Having served on several murder squads during my police service, I am aware of the procedures the police follow in such investigations and the manner in which they are carried out, albeit under strict rules.

On that night they had two people in custody, both of whom appeared to be responsible for or involved in the death of their son, and the matter had to be investigated fully. From the outset, Andy said very little to the police other than that Jacob's death was a 'mercy killing'. He was immediately represented at the police station by his solicitor, who advised him to say nothing, which was his right, and that advice was later confirmed as correct by Andy's barrister.

Mary, on the other hand, was questioned by the police and, over a period of two days, made at least two lengthy statements. She probably fully expected that Andy would make a statement and say that she was not involved in Jacob's death, but because he had been advised to say nothing, that was to come later. The police presumably would have wished for a confession from Mary implicating herself, if she was involved, and Andy, or a statement from Andy exonerating her, but they had neither.

On her release, Mary told me that if he continued to say nothing and unless he changed his solicitor, Andy would be facing life imprisonment. She told me that this reasoning was suggested to her while she was in custody, by the police and her solicitor. She was so adamant about it that when she spoke to Andy on the phone a few days later while he was on remand in Lewes Prison, she insisted he change his solicitor – he, wisely, did not do so.

The pressure on Mary was enormous, she had lost her beloved Jacob and she was now facing the prospect of being charged with being complicit in his death. If, as Andy has always maintained, he and Mary had agreed on a course of action that would not implicate her, she was understandably desperate to exonerate herself after three days in custody. She would also have been worried about George. Mary thus made a statement saying she had no knowledge of what Andy was going to do, not realizing, as she said later, that she would be required to give evidence against him.

Andy and Mary were somewhat naive if they thought that by Mary being absent from the house when Andy ended Jacob's life, but knowing that it was going to happen, then Mary could not be implicated. However, it seems that the fact that Mary could be a prosecution witness had never occurred to him.

When I visited Andy when he was on remand in Lewes, the first thing he told me was that Mary had agreed with ending Jacob's life and that she was aware of what was going to happen on that night. However, he told me under no circumstances did he want Mary implicated because, should she be charged with either murder or conspiracy to murder, the consequences for George would be catastrophic. He could be deprived of both parents and even placed in care.

From the outset, Andy wanted to protect Mary. Indeed, he did not even tell his legal team that Mary was involved until he realized that she was going to give evidence against him.

The day after she was released, Mary came to see Anne and me, and while at our house she spoke to Andy, who was still in prison, on the phone. After finishing that phone call, Anne, Steve, who was also present, and myself were all very surprised when Mary expressed to us her wishes that Andy should remain in prison and be refused bail. She said she loved him but feared for his mental wellbeing if he was free.

She told me that she had taken George out of the house late at night, both of them saying 'goodbye' to Jacob. She had left Jacob alone in the house for a few minutes, knowing Andy was soon coming back. Mary told me that she had told the police that the reason she had woken George and left the house at eleven o'clock at night was to take him to her mother's, in order that she and Andy could enjoy a night of sex. She said that she had felt embarrassed to tell the police this. Mary gave that explanation in her evidence to the court and whether she was believed or not is probably irrelevant because she wasn't on trial, but at the conclusion of the case it was evident from the Judge's sentencing remarks that she certainly did not.

Mary admitted in her evidence that she had been drinking and should not have driven, but on taking George out of the house, and prior to taking him to her mother's, she sat in her car and drank from a bottle of wine. She received a phone call from Andy telling her that he had ended their son's life. After dropping George off at her mother's, she returned to the house where Andy was waiting and cuddling the lifeless body of Jacob. Andy wanted to phone the police immediately but Mary said she persuaded him to join her with a glass of wine and drink 'a toast' to Jacob, now he was released from his suffering. Mary was questioned about that, particularly as she stated that she had no knowledge of what Andy was going to do, and that it had been a shock when she arrived home and saw that he had ended Jacob's life.

On 29 July, Steve, Chris and Sara spent the evening at Mary's and they talked long into the night. Both Steve and Chris later commented that they found it strange that Mary said nothing detrimental about Andy, which one might have expected if he had ended Jacob's life against her wishes.

When all these facts are taken into account it is hardly surprising that Mary found herself in a great dilemma. She could not go back on her explanation to the police for fear of being charged. Under English Law, a wife cannot be compelled to give evidence against her husband. Whether Mary was informed of that, by her solicitor or the police, I do not know. At the time of Jacob's death, Mary and Andy were still married. However, by the time of the trial she had divorced him and subsequently gave evidence for the prosecution.

The police did briefly interview Anne and me, but we informed them that we could not assist them regarding Jacob's death and would only speak to Andrew's solicitor as we were likely to be witnesses in his defence. Anne did give evidence but I did not as it was felt that I could add nothing of relevance to the case.

Andy appeared at Lewes Crown Court on Thursday 5 August 2004, before His Hon. Judge Richard Brown. He was represented by Mr Oscar Vincent, his solicitor, and Mr Timothy Mousley, QC. The charge was put to Andy that he had murdered Jacob and he confirmed that he understood. He was not asked to enter a plea to the charge and the solicitor for the Crown Prosecution Service briefly outlined the circumstances of Jacob's death. Mr Timothy Mousley informed the Court that Andy would eventually plead not guilty to the charge of murder. On being told that the case would be adjourned until 22 October, the defence lawyer addressed the judge regarding the question of bail. He referred to the prison reports and stated that Andy, if granted bail, would not be a danger to himself or anyone else and he would be willing to abide by any bail conditions that the court laid down.

After some deliberation, Judge Brown agreed to grant Andy bail with the following conditions: he was not to reside in or enter West Sussex except to see his son, George, and under supervision; he was not to contact Mary or other prosecution witnesses; he was to surrender his passport; he was to reside at an address approved by the police; and he was to provide two sureties of £50,000. Andy of course agreed to all these conditions. Chris and Sara agreed that Andy could live with them in Wimbledon while awaiting trial, and Anne and I agreed to provide the sureties.

There was a mass of press reporters, photographers and television crews outside the court and Andy later told me that it was only when he saw them that he fully realized how much media interest there was in the case. Chris and I had parked our cars about two minutes' walk from the court and the police advised us that the best way of dealing with the press was to give them a statement, otherwise they would follow us to the cars and beyond.

We all waited at the rear of the building and after thirty minutes Andy emerged, accompanied by Oscar Vincent. As he came through the gates he went straight to Anne, put his arms around her and held her tightly. She was crying and I heard her say, 'I love you, Andy.' He then hugged Tina, Chris, Sara and myself.

The press surged forward, shouting questions, flashguns going off in our faces. It seemed to go on forever – we were absolutely surrounded. Andy's solicitor then made a short statement to the media in which he said: 'Andy is immensely relieved to be granted bail. It will allow him to spend time with his family, grieve properly for the loss of Jacob and deal with the funeral arrangements.' Unfortunately, most of that turned out not to be possible.

The police were right, the reporters were happy with the statement – a few of them did follow us to our cars but we said nothing and two policemen accompanied us most of the way to the car park. Andy, Chris and Sara drove off to Wimbledon, Anne, Tina and I returned to Worthing. When Anne and I arrived at our house, a reporter from a national newspaper was waiting, he was polite and friendly but we told him that we did not wish to make any statement or answer questions. He understood and left his card, should we wish to give him our story sometime in the future.

The next day, Anne and I drove to Wimbledon to visit Andy and to pick up Sara's mother, Rev. Vicki Hammel, who had flown in from America and, at Mary's request, was to officiate at Jacob's funeral. Andy was understandably fairly subdued, and before we left he spent about an hour in private talking to and being counselled by Vicki, who had met Jacob once before on a previous visit to England. Andy later told me that the time he spent with Vicki was invaluable.

On that same day, Andy gave his permission for Jacob's body to be released for burial. Two autopsies had already been carried out and Andy's defence team wanted another as they thought it might help his case for some reason. He went against their advice and was quite adamant that there should be no further delay, for Mary's sake and in order that the funeral could take place as soon as possible.

Prior to us arriving at Chris's house in Wimbledon, a reporter from a national newspaper had called at the house and informed Andy that they were printing a story in their Sunday edition involving an affair Andy had had sometime previously, at a time when he was separated from Mary, and asking him if he wanted to make a comment. Andy obviously declined, but he did phone Mary to warn her of what might be in the Sunday paper and one can imagine the understandable reaction that provoked. In the event nothing appeared in the paper that weekend.

Anne, Vicki and I returned to Worthing that evening and sat in the quiet of our home discussing the recent events involving our children long into the night. Vicki is a wonderful person and I am sure she would not mind me describing her as 'not a typical vicar'. She is kind and understanding, not patronizing in any way and is the first to admit that she does not have an answer to everything that happens to us in our lives.

The following day, Vicki went to Mary's for dinner and to plan Jacob's Remembrance Service and funeral. Andy had no input into the services whatsoever and said he was not consulted by Mary, although I am sure Vicki informed him of the plans.

Andy's birthday, 8 August, came and went. I think the family sent him cards but there was no celebration.

Over the next few days, Vicki liaised with Mary and they went to Chestnut Tree House to finalize the arrangements for the Remembrance

Service. Mary evidently did not want Andy to be at the service and in the end he thought it would be best if he didn't go. However, they did agree that he should meet her and Vicki at Jacob's graveside for a private burial.

By this time Jacob had been taken to the bereavement room at Chestnut Tree Hospice. Andy obtained permission of the court to come down from London and, on 14 August, Andy, Chris and I went to the hospice.

I just cannot describe my feelings as we waited to see Jacob. Nobody can ever know that feeling in the stomach if they have not experienced it. Chris and I waited as Andy went to be with his son. He spent quite some time with him, about half an hour I think, and when he rejoined us he looked pale and in shock, upset and moved. He said nothing and Chris and I left him to his own thoughts as we went to see Jacob.

The room was very cool and it was arranged as a child's bedroom. Our precious little boy was lying in a bed, wearing his Chelsea shirt and cap. He looked so very peaceful and it was obvious that he was no longer in any sort of pain. He was surrounded by several of his toys and cards. Chris and I went to either side of the bed, held Jacob's hand and kissed his forehead. We said very little to each other, fought back the tears and agreed that we were both so relieved that he was no longer suffering. We said goodbye to our beloved little boy, who had been such a large part of our lives, given us so many happy memories and, on reflection, taught us so much. Chris and I agreed that we were so glad that we had seen Jacob.

Before we left the hospice Andy went back to say his private goodbye to his son.

Andy and Chris returned to Wimbledon and Chris later told me that Andy related to him exactly what had happened between him and Mary in the days leading up to Jacob's death and on the day it happened. Those details were later to be revealed in Andy's trial.

On 15 August, Steve flew back from Washington and the next day, the day of the funeral, he also visited Jacob at Chestnut Tree Hospice, prior to the Remembrance Service. Unfortunately his wife, Carmen, had had to stay at home in Washington to look after their children while Steve made two trips to England. She told me that she would have liked to have travelled over with Steve but I know he was grateful for the love and support she gave him from a distance.

Monday 16 August 2004, another day we will never forget. It was agreed that Andy should come to Worthing with Chris and Sara and stay at our house for the duration of the Remembrance Service at Chestnut Tree House. I would then take him to the churchyard to meet Mary and Vicki for Jacob's burial; I would not stay for the burial itself but would pick him up afterwards. Originally, I did not want to leave Andy alone in our house while we were all at the service, however, he assured me that he would be all right and insisted I went.

There were about 150 people at the service. Friends had travelled long distances from all over the country and beyond. Mary and Andy had been friendly with the mother of a lovely boy, TJ, who had also suffered from MPS. TJ and his family lived in South Africa and had met Andy, Mary, Jacob and George a few years earlier when they were visiting England. Sadly, TJ had died but his mother came over for Jacob's service. A couple they were friendly with who had two young boys who also suffered from Hunter Syndrome, travelled with their sons from their home in the north of England to be at the service, and the two boys sat in the front row with George. I wondered what their parents must have thought, sitting through the service knowing that they faced the almost inevitable prospect of losing both their precious boys sometime in the not-too-distant future. Later, I learnt, the couple separated, such was the strain they were under. What a cruel world this is.

The room in which the service was held was decorated with numerous photographs, some greatly enlarged, of Jacob during various stages of his life. The Order of Service showed a beautiful photo of our grandson with Mickey Mouse. Vicki conducted the service and I thought it wonderful that she opened it by directly addressing George and his two friends, sitting at the front. She asked them if they knew why they were there and they confirmed that they knew they were remembering Jacob and the happy times he had shared with everyone.

We said the 'Twenty-third Psalm' and sang Jacob's favourite, 'Barney's Song' and, just for Jacob, I want to repeat it here:

I love you, you love me
We're a happy family
With a great big hug
And a kiss from me to you

Won't you say you love me too?

I love you, you love me
We're best friends as friends should be
With a great big hug
And a kiss from me to you
Won't you say you love me too?

It was difficult to sing through the tears but we did it, just for Jacob. Towards the end of the service, Vicki, with Mary's agreement, had allowed for anyone who wished to remember Jacob to say whatever they wanted. I had written a poem in memory of our grandson and Andy had agreed to me reading it. I knew it was going to be very difficult for me to get through it without breaking down but I also knew I had to do it for Jacob. Steve had agreed to read the poem if I felt I could not and I thank him so much for his wonderful gesture as I know he would have found it as difficult as I did.

When Vicki invited anyone who wished to to say a few words, nobody did – perhaps everyone felt too emotional. I waited a few seconds and walked to the front of the congregation. After saying a few words about Jacob being 'Happy' all his life and wanting everyone else to be 'Happy' and telling the story about him putting his hearing aid in the microwave, I read my poem.

Jacob Our Grandson
Jacob, our darling beautiful lovely boy,
You have given Nannie and Grandad such wonderful joy.
Your smile and your hugs we will never forget
You gave so much love to those who you met.
You can now be happy with the friends who you love,
With Barnie, Willie and Pingu, you will see us all from above.
You are Henry's big brother and our hearts will not ache,
Because the Wragg brothers are together, what a team you will make.
We will miss you so much in our own special way
But we know from now on you'll have such a 'Busy Day'.
Chris, Sara, Steve, Carmen, Noel, Chelsea, Tina, Max and Ella,
All their love will be with you forever and ever.
HAPPY Nannie, HAPPY Grandad, big hugs from us to you,
Goodbye Darling Jacob, we'll remember your special big hugs too.

When I started to read the poem Mary left her seat and walked out of the room, I hesitated a second but carried on. Andy later told me that when he met Mary at the graveside she told him that I had ruined the Remembrance Service and Vicki confirmed what she had said. I was very surprised by her comments, couldn't understand it and at the time felt quite hurt. I know the poem is not going to win any prizes but it was written shortly after Jacob died and reflects my – and Anne's – feelings. I acknowledge that Mary was in turmoil on that day and she was entitled to her opinion but I will never understand how my words upset her and I am sorry that they did. Having gone through the funeral of our baby Joanne many years ago I can relate to some of the feelings Mary and Andy were going through on that day. I asked Andy to ensure that the poem, along with Jacob's favourite book, My Busy Day, that his Nannie used to read to him, was buried with him. He told me that they were.

I returned home immediately after the service and took Andy to the churchyard. I did not wait but the car carrying Jacob arrived after a few minutes. Andy joined Mary and Vicki at the graveside and the parents requested that the coffin be opened in order that they could say goodbye to their beloved son one last time. This was done and several personal items were placed in the coffin including Andy's SAS belt, for which he had worked so hard. Vicki conducted a short service and our Jacob was laid to rest in peace in Durrington Cemetery, Worthing, high on a hill overlooking the South Downs.

Mary returned to the Hospice, where everyone had remained while the burial took place. Steve, Chris and several of the aunts, uncles and cousins entertained George and the other children. George later told me that he had a great time playing football with Steve and Chris. He was not to know that it would be over two years before he was allowed to see either of his uncles again.

A short time later I went with Andy to a local pub where most of the family joined us. We stayed for a couple of hours before everyone went their separate ways, Vicki and Steve returning to America the next day. Andy went back to London with Chris and Sara to prepare for his trial.

The police had said that they would be at the cemetery to prevent any press intervention – I think a police car was there. Even so one enterprising photographer managed to evade them and the next day a photograph of Andy, Mary and Vicki standing by the graveside appeared in the Sun newspaper. In fairness to them, they did ask Andy's solicitor if he would give permission for the photo to be published and Andy agreed on condition that the paper made a donation to Chestnut Tree House, which I believe they did.

Under normal circumstances that should have been the closing of a chapter. We always knew that we were going to lose Jacob; that had happened, and we should have been able to retreat quietly into our individual lives and grieved our loss in our own ways. But it did not happen for any of us. Andy was facing possible life imprisonment and it was only the beginning of a very traumatic and stressful sixteen months.

Chapter 6
Awaiting Trial

It's hard to imagine Andy's state of mind as he awaited trial. It was, however, a consolation that he was staying with Chris and Sara in Wimbledon – the alternative was for him to live in a bail hostel, which none of us wanted.

He had been told that while on bail he could see George under supervision, and his solicitor said he would arrange it. However, Mary objected, so unfortunately that never came about and Andy was not able to see George for nearly three years. On 13 January 2005 Andy applied at Worthing Family Court for access to George. The application failed on the grounds that Mary was still concerned about George's safety, and the Judge decided he could not hear the case and adjourned it to the Family High Court in London – which meant yet another interminable delay.

The first hearing at the Family Court in London was not until 25 July 2005, when Mary again objected to Andy seeing George, on the grounds that Andy could be a danger to his son. She said that George might be frightened that if he became ill Andy might kill him. Of course it was right that Mary should have George's safety as a priority but as time went on we could never understand why the Family Court appeared to ignore the recommendations of social workers, the Children and Family Court Advisory and Support Service (CAFCASS) and psychiatrists. Indeed, one psychiatrist stated that in his opinion Andy posed no threat to anyone, least of all George, and he could not understand why Andy had not been allowed to see George under supervision for such a long time. Despite this, Mary disagreed and the Family Court kept postponing their decision for various reasons: reports weren't ready, witnesses were on holiday or did not appear.

On one occasion a bereavement counsellor was asked to submit a report on George and the case was postponed for nearly three months in order that she could do so. When the Family Court reconvened, the counsellor failed to produce a report and stated that it was not in her remit to do so. That may well have been true but one might have thought that the Family Court could have been informed earlier. The result was a further delay of three months for more reports to be submitted. One thing that was obvious from this was the lack of funds and staff within the social services sector, which caused delay after delay and went on for over two and a half years. Having seen what Andy experienced, I certainly have a great deal of sympathy with the Fathers for Justice Campaign. Andy was so frustrated that on several occasions he even said that his life would not be worth living if he could not see George. He tried to keep in touch, sending George cards and presents, but he was never certain if he received them.

In addition to the distress of not seeing his son, Andy found it extremely difficult to find employment. He attended several interviews but every time he explained that he was on bail, he received sympathy but no offer of work. Andy has always been a hard worker and never unemployed, he went to several building sites to get casual work but with no result. He was offered jobs by friends in Worthing but because of his bail conditions was unable to take up the offers. Another problem was that he had to attend conferences with his legal team in London, which made it more difficult for him to take a permanent job. He did eventually obtain part-time employment with a security company and worked in a London hotel and at other various locations.

The pressure of all this very soon built up and began to cause problems between Chris, Sara and Andy. Andy started to drink heavily, which produced a dilemma for Chris: his brother was on bail for murder, could not see his son, and was out of work. Chris was married and possibly felt torn between the love of his wife and the responsibility of looking after his brother. He did not want to go out every night drinking with Andy – and I doubt that Andy expected him to. But Chris was concerned that if Andy became drunk, he might end up in trouble even if it was not his fault. Andy would sometimes arrive home late, quite drunk, and fall asleep in the living room. He would then wake up during the night and Sara recalls how she once heard him sobbing loudly and saying 'Jacob, Jacob'. She comforted him and he went to bed.

Occasionally, some of Andy's friends from Worthing went to Wimbledon to take him out, which was kind of them, and he did manage to fit in the odd game of golf. Chris and I also played golf with him but he just was not his usual self. He would lose his temper over something silly, on one occasion deliberately breaking one of his clubs and storming off the course, an action totally out of character as far as I was concerned. He met Chris and me back at the club house and apologized but it was very evident that all was not well.

Andy later told me that he felt guilty about the pressure his presence put on Chris and Sara and he will always be grateful to them for allowing him to stay with them while he was on bail. They were both working long hours and doing their best to get on with their lives, whereas his life was on hold, with a very uncertain future. He said that although he was with some of his family it was one of his unhappiest, loneliest and most depressing times of his life, as he had no control whatsoever over the circumstances and situation in which he found himself.

Anne and I visited Wimbledon fairly regularly and went out for meals with Andy, Chris and Sara. Once our daughter Tina visited him and when they were out Andy told her he would not want to go on living if he couldn't see George.

Andy continued to have regular conferences with his legal team, which had by then been finalized. His original barrister was unable to take the case and he was replaced by one of the country's leading QCs, Mr Michael Sayers. His solicitor was Mr Chris Hayes and his assistant was a fantastic young Crown case worker called Louise Colwell, who was, at the time, studying for her legal exams. She worked unbelievably hard throughout and was responsible for ensuring that the case was presented to Mr Sayers in a truly professional way. I would have liked to have been present to support Andy at those conferences but was not allowed as there was a chance I could be a witness for the defence. However, it was agreed at an early stage that Andy could be accompanied and advised by another close family member who was very experienced in prosecutions and criminal cases. He gave Andy great support at every conference and throughout the trials and both Andy and I will always be indebted to him for the work he did and the time he gave.

Andy appeared at Lewes Crown Court again on 22 October 2004, but the case was adjourned until 12 November, as more time was needed to consider the evidence. Andy was told that his bail conditions would be extended but in addition he was not to contact his wife, including text messages and phone calls. Anne and I were also instructed by Andy's lawyers that we, and other family members, should have no contact with Mary or any other possible prosecution witnesses, as it could jeopardize Andy's case.

On 12 November, Andy was arraigned and pleaded not guilty to the charge of murder. The date for his trial was set for 28 February 2005, with a preliminary hearing on 18 January. After leaving court, Andy was given permission to go to Worthing with Chris and Sara, where they placed flowers on Jacob's grave.

At the pre-trial hearing on 18 January the Judge instructed the prosecution that they must give a decision regarding an alternative charge of manslaughter by 22 January, as Andy had received two psychiatric reports for his defence and indicated that he would plead 'Guilty' to that charge on the grounds of diminished responsibility. That instruction was delayed, however, as the prosecution requested their own psychiatrist's report on Andy and it was not possible for that to be done until 25 January. As Andy had been on bail and available for medical examination since August 2004, this delay was infuriating and we were all kept on tenterhooks once more. When it came, the prosecution's psychiatric report was distressing in that it did not consider Andy was suffering from diminished responsibility when he ended Jacob's life.

The devastating news that the Crown Prosecution Service would not accept a plea to manslaughter and were proceeding to trial on the charge of murder came through on 10 February.

Andy seemed quite philosophical, as he had been told by his lawyers to 'expect the worst', but we were very disappointed. We now knew that we had to come to terms with the fact that in three weeks' time a long murder trial involving our son was going to take place and we would have to face the heartache and stress it would bring, not to mention all the media interest.

For our part, from the moment Andy was granted bail our lives in Worthing were dominated by the preparation and anticipation of his trial, which was made more difficult by not knowing exactly when it would be. Immediately following our son's arrest we were subjected to intense media interest.

From the first day it was impossible for Anne and me to go shopping without seeing newspaper hoardings with glaring headlines about Jacob's death and his parents' arrest. Every national and local paper carried photographs of them and it was the lead story on television and radio news. It affected Anne greatly and she only left the house when she had to.

We knew that there would be difficult times ahead but we had no idea exactly how difficult. Within just a few days, while Andy was in prison, we were to find out. A couple of days after Andy was remanded in custody, Anne wrote a card to Mary saying how sorry and sad she was and 'As one mother to another', no matter what had happened and what might happen, could Mary just spare a moment to think of Andy in prison as he loved her and his children so much and was hurting terribly.

A couple of days after posting that card I answered the door to two police officers who wanted to speak to Anne. She had been on night duty at the hospital and was sleeping. The officers would not tell me why they wanted to see her but said they would call back. When she awoke, Anne was naturally very worried. The police called back later that day. They produced the card Anne had sent to Mary and asked her to confirm that she had sent it, which she readily did. They then informed her that in view of the fact that Mary could well be a prosecution witness, which Anne did not know at that time, the card could be viewed as an attempt to put pressure on Mary and influence her, and if that was the case then Anne could be seen as 'attempting to pervert the course of justice'.

We were absolutely stunned. I was aware that one should not approach a prosecution witness but this seemed ridiculous in the extreme, particularly as we did not know at that early stage that Mary would be a witness. The two officers actually said that they had been instructed by their senior officer to come round and 'warn' Anne not to approach Mary in future, or she might be arrested, adding that they felt 'slightly embarrassed' at having to do so.

Not approaching Mary if she was to be a prosecution witness was understandable but from that moment it was obvious that we would have to avoid any kind of contact whatsoever. That presented a number of problems and on several occasions I took advice and instructions from Andy's solicitor.

A charity football match was arranged in Worthing to raise money in memory of Jacob for the Hospice – I am not sure who arranged it – and a local team played a team comprising ex-Chelsea players. It was agreed that George should kick the game off. I would have loved to have gone to the game but on legal advice did not. We were all told that we should not put ourselves in any situation where we would be likely to come into contact with Mary. Although we would not obviously confront her, we should not be in a position where she could confront us. It was not suggested that we would discuss anything to do with the case but, in view of what had happened with the card Anne had sent, it was essential that no situation should arise where allegations could be made about influencing witnesses.

It was a sad situation and whatever we might have thought of Mary's behaviour, we found ourselves in a position over which we had no control and we knew that even one small incident involving ourselves and a prosecution witness could be totally misinterpreted.

We only lived two miles from Mary and Anne and I were concerned that it was possible we could bump into her and George while shopping in Worthing. Our legal advice was to try and avoid them, cross the road, if possible, or at the most just say 'Hello' to George and walk on; make a note of what had happened and inform Andy's solicitor of the incident. Luckily the situation did not arise with us; however, it did with Tina.

On the day before the first trial, Tina was shopping in Worthing with our granddaughter Ella, George's cousin, when she saw Mary and George approaching. In view of some of the text messages she had previously received from Mary concerning Andy, and particularly given the legal advice we had received, Tina did not want to speak to her and crossed the road. Tina does not know if Mary saw her but it was a sad incident as the two girls had always got on reasonably well.

On Jacob's birthday, Anne and I visited Jacob's grave and placed some roses from our garden from ourselves and Andy. There were also flowers and cards from Mary and George, and from Gwen, Jacob's other grandmother. I revisited the grave two days later and pretty well all the flowers were gone, at least the heads of the flowers had gone only the stems were left! I spoke to two gravediggers who were working in the graveyard and they told me that there was a family of deer living close by and they loved fresh flowers. Looking around the graveyard I could see why many graves had been covered in various ways. When I suggested to Anne that in future we should only place plastic flowers on the grave, she disagreed and said that on the contrary, we would always place fresh ones, so that the deer could have their fun. Jacob would think it funny that the deer were 'pinching' his flowers and he would be happy. To this day we always lay fresh flowers for Jacob and the deer.

We do not visit the grave a great deal, only on Jacob's birthday and special days. Anne always says she doesn't need a grave to remember our grandson – we have many happy memories that we recall every day.

However when we did go in the early days after Jacob's death, we always made sure that we went at a time when we thought Mary would be picking up George from school, thus avoiding a potential meeting there.

The question of Jacob's grave has presented a dilemma for Andy over the past three years. As I understand it, nothing can be done regarding the placing of a headstone on a grave for at least two years, by which time the ground will have settled. For some time, Andy has been keen to arrange for a headstone to be placed but in view of the fact that the grave is owned by the person who purchased the plot and arranged the burial – Mary – he has to liaise with her for it to be done, which has proved difficult. However, it seems the headstone is finally going to be put in place as a lasting memory.

After one of the remand hearings at court, when Andy was given permission to visit Jacob's grave, he was shocked at the condition. It was partially overgrown with weeds. I went with him to a garden centre and he bought several bags of small grey stones and an anti-weed covering to place under them. We took some garden tools from home and went back to the graveyard. As we arrived at the grave, tears came to my eyes as Andy bent over, started removing the weeds, and said to Jacob, 'OK, son. Let's get you sorted out.' When Andy had finished, Jacob's resting place looked much better and has remained so ever since.

One small event that occurred shortly after Jacob's death did affect me at the time. I have to attend Worthing Hospital on a regular basis to receive blood transfusions for a condition I have. One such visit was scheduled for a few days after Jacob died but prior to his funeral. The department that I go to is on the first floor of the hospital and immediately below that floor is the mortuary. As I approached the stairs leading up to the haematology department, I walked past a sign saying 'Hospital Mortuary and Coroner'. I had walked past that sign on several occasions, but on that particular day it was different, because I knew that a post-mortem was being carried out on my beloved grandson in the mortuary.

I am reminded of Jacob and that sad day every time I go to the hospital for a transfusion. However, I cheer myself up because I also walk past the audiology department where Jacob was a patient and I have a smile as I remember him being fitted with his hearing aid and later cooking it and setting fire to the microwave. No matter what sad memories come to mind regarding Jacob there is always a happy one that can be recalled.

From the very beginning of this terrible episode in our lives, Anne and I, Andy and the rest of the family received wonderful support and love from many people, some of whom we had never met and did not know. We received about two hundred cards and letters from all over the world, including America, Canada, Australia and South Africa. Anne managed to reply to many of them and we apologize to those kind people who did not hear from us – your support and compassionate words meant a great deal to us and we will always be indebted to you for boosting our morale during those dark days. We also heard from some old friends with whom we had lost touch and I even heard from someone I went to school with. I was always very touched by the friends who phoned us – we all know how hard it is to find words when talking to someone who has just lost a loved one, and to do so given the dreadful circumstances Anne and I found ourselves in must have been so much harder.

Support also came from unexpected sources. We received a letter offering any help we needed from our Member of Parliament, Mr Peter Bottomley; also a beautiful bouquet of flowers from Philip Schofield and Fern Britton who present the morning television programme. Our neighbours were tremendous. Like many typical English folk, all leading busy lives, we hardly knew some of the families living near us, only those no more than a few doors away. However, we were amazed at the number of folk who put cards through our door, or spoke to us in the street, expressing their feelings and wishing us luck. I also heard from several of the pupils I had taught to drive when I was a driving instructor.

In the early days we did not know that Mary would become so bitter, but we soon realized that she probably would not support Andrew. Many people would enquire how Andy and Mary were coping and it was difficult to answer for Mary as we were not allowed to talk to her. I can honestly say that we did not receive one word of criticism about Andy, written or otherwise, during those times. That was to come later in some newspapers and on websites.

Christmas 2004 approached and none of us were looking forward to it. Chris and Sara went to Boston to spend a well-deserved holiday with Sara's family. Anne and I stayed at home and enjoyed the days as best we could with Tina, Max and our granddaughter Ella. We put up our decorations with little enthusiasm, but Ella lifted our spirits with the typical excitement of childhood. Andy was not allowed to come to Worthing, which seemed extremely harsh, and although we offered to join him in Wimbledon, he declined and said he would rather be alone. I wasn't happy with this idea, but agreed, and I still do not know how he spent that Christmas Day.

We have a fairly large extended family and in addition to Anne and myself, George has a great-grandmother, many aunts, uncles and cousins whom he has known all his life. On their birthdays and at Christmas both he and Jacob would receive presents from most of them. This year, as usual, we, Andy and many other members of the family, bought Christmas presents for George. By the time Anne had collected the presents from everyone it was getting very close to Christmas and we did not want to post them. I contacted the Police Family Liaison Officer, who suggested that I should not go to Mary's house but instead contact the social services, and if they could not deliver the presents, then he would do so. Andy was furious that I had spoken to the police and I have never understood why, as I was only trying to solve the problem. Louise Colwell from Andy's solicitors arranged for me to give the presents to a social worker, and on 23 December I delivered them to their offices. We have never heard but I presume George received all his presents from Father Christmas.

I spent all Christmas Eve having a blood transfusion and I can honestly say that I was quite pleased to lie on the hospital bed all day and rest. The nurses and staff in the Day Care Unit have always been wonderful in their treatment of me but from the very first moment they knew of the trauma I was experiencing in my life they were magnificent.

I do not normally keep a diary but from the time of Jacob's death I did so, not with the intention of writing a book but in anticipation that I might be called as a witness sometime and I wanted an accurate record of events as they affected me. While I was having the blood transfusion, I spent the time updating my diary and one of the nursing sisters, Kathy, asked me what I was writing. She was sympathetic and suggested that getting everything down on paper would prove to be therapeutic – and she was right, it did. Kathy told me that she had lost a young child after a long illness at Christmastime a year earlier and she had written a book about her family's sad experiences. She later gave me her book to read and although it was sad it was a beautiful record of love and courage but above all a tribute to, and memory of, Kathy's child.

On Christmas evening, back at home, I received a text message from Andy, which I kept on my mobile phone for over a year and which meant so much to Anne and me. It read 'Happy Xmas, Mum and Dad, I love you so much. Thanks for everything.' He has never been one to show or express his emotions and Anne and I both agreed that the text was the best Christmas present we could have received.

Then it was New Year's Eve. I can't remember what Anne and I did, I think we probably just spent the evening at home together, we certainly did not celebrate. We were obviously wished a 'Happy New Year' by many people over the next few days and we agreed that this year above all others, we wanted those words to come true, nothing could be as bad as the previous year had been.

Between Christmas and the trial at the end of February, Andy was occupied with going to Worthing Family Court to apply for access to George, seeing the prosecution psychiatrist and attending numerous conferences in London with his legal team to finalize details of his trial and prepare his defence. I travelled up to meet him after two of those conferences and, together with a family friend who was advising him throughout, we talked about the forthcoming trial over sandwiches and not a few beers.

Andy seemed quite positive about the way his legal team had prepared him for the weeks ahead, the weeks that would define his future life. He was realistic though, and had been told, once again, to expect the worst. If found guilty of murder, he would go to prison for life and probably serve about fifteen years; if found guilty of manslaughter – to which he was prepared to plead guilty if the prosecution accepted it – he might receive a sentence of about five years. Andy always said that he expected to be punished according to the law and anything less than a five-year term of imprisonment was a bonus. He was ready to serve any term of imprisonment for Jacob.

We sat in the pub for several hours, talking about all these scenarios and no matter how bleak the future looked Andy never lost his dry sense of humour. He often talked about Jacob and frequently said he knew he had done the right thing in ending Jacob's suffering. He had more or less anticipated everything that had happened to him since Jacob's death and was prepared for it, but he was shocked and upset that Mary had not continued to support him and had obstructed him from seeing George under supervision. Even on that subject Andy's humour showed when he said he wanted nothing more than to see his son, even just to kick a ball about with him and he was quite happy for the whole of Sussex Police, the SAS and the band of the Welsh Guards to be there for George's supervision and security if that made Mary happy!

The date for the start of the trial approached and Anne and I seemed to get less and less sleep. We would go to bed fairly late but it made no difference, most nights we got up during the night, drank tea and looked at the television, not watching anything. How do you occupy yourself when the countdown has begun for you to face the most traumatic events of your life? I couldn't imagine what Andy was going through, or Mary, knowing that she was shortly to give evidence against him.

Chapter 7

The First Trial: The Case for the Prosecution

Lewes is the County Town of East Sussex, about fifteen miles from Brighton and near the coast. The town boasts a long history, which is reflected in many of its old buildings, narrow streets and antique shops. Over the centuries, justice was dispensed at several locations in Lewes and in 1761 a stone and brick building was erected more or less on the site of the present courthouse, opposite the White Hart Inn. That building remained until it was replaced in 1812 at its current location. Over the years, much repair work and alteration has been carried out and eventually, on 27 January 1995, after being closed for approximately two years, the courthouse reopened as we see it today.

From the eighteenth century, records still exist bearing the names of hundreds of convicted felons who were tried at Lewes Assizes and deported to the British Colonies, many for the offence of smuggling. Since then the Assizes, later to become the Crown Court, has seen many famous trials, some of which resulted in the death sentence. One of the most notorious was probably that of John George Haigh, known as the 'acid bath murderer', who was sentenced to death at his trial in Lewes and subsequently hanged at Wandsworth prison in 1949.

The death sentence for the crime of murder was abolished in English law in 1969. Until that date, when a judge was passing sentence a black cap – which was in fact a three-cornered piece of silk – was placed over the judge's wig. The practice was very ancient and regarded as a sign of mourning and examples of black headwear being used in this way occurs in the Scriptures, in the classics and in modern literature. The black cap is to the present day part of a judge's regalia, and although there is no need for it to be worn, it is still carried by High Court judges. A strange custom one might think.

Interestingly, although often seen in films and television programmes and mentioned in almost everything else involving judges, the one place you won't see a gavel is in an English or Welsh courtroom – they are not used there.

The court building itself is quite unimpressive from the outside: it has the appearance of any town hall or public building and houses several courts. The Number One Court, where Andy's trial took place, though, is very impressive and imposing. It has been restored to its original grandeur with a grant from National Heritage and the result is magnificent. I have been in many courts in my time with the Metropolitan Police, the most impressive of which is probably Number One Court at the Old Bailey in London. However, I think the Court at Lewes runs it a close second, and I once heard a leading QC agree with that. I doubt that many who enter the dock have thoughts about admiring their surroundings or the history attached to them, though.

The Judge selected to try Andy's case was High Court Judge, Her Honour Mrs Justice Anne Rafferty. She has been described by journalists and some in the legal profession as 'impressive and a mixture of traditional and radical.' In one article Anne Rafferty was described as ,a million miles from the stereotypical image of a judge – a reactionary Old Etonian in his late 70's who would not know his Eminem from his M & S.'

Her Honour was educated at Sheffield University, called to the Bar in 1974 and, following a distinguished career prosecuting and defending in high profile cases, was appointed High Court Judge in 2002. She evidently has strong opinions on the British criminal justice system which was evident in an interview in 2002 in which she stated that the general public often formed the opinion, wrongly, that defendants had "got off" based on the distorted way cases were reported in the newspapers. She thinks wigs and gowns should still be worn in court. She also stated in the 2002 interview that she is in favour of the abolition of the mandatory life sentence for murder. "Don't tell me that a man who lurkes in the bushes and knifes a 16 year old girl on her way home, and an 82 year old pensioner who puts a pillow over the face of his terminally ill wife because he cannot bear to see her suffer deserves the same sentence." She added that she believed that judges should be free to give people who commit premeditated killings anything from a suspended sentence to natural life imprisonment. Poignant remarks, perhaps.

The first trial commenced on Monday 28 February 2005, before Her Honour Mrs Justice Rafferty. It was a cold day and snow was falling heavily. The prosecution was led by Mr Philip Katz, QC, an experienced Crown prosecutor and Andy's defence team consisted of Mr Michael Sayers, QC, Mr Tony Bailey and Ms Louise Colwell. Mr Sayers is a very experienced lawyer having defended in many high profile cases. He has also often sat as a Judge/Recorder at the Old Bailey. Standing very erect, well over six feet tall, with long grey hair showing under his wig he exuded an air of professionalism and confidence. I later heard that shortly after defending Andy Mr Sayers retired from the Bar.

The court sat Monday to Friday from 10.00 a.m. until approximately 4.30 p.m. on most days, and the case lasted for three weeks.

Andy waited with us, his family, in the witness waiting room until the case was called. Those who were going to be witnesses waited there until they were called to give evidence –, in some cases they had to wait for several days before being called, after which they were allowed to remain in court. I was not giving evidence and sat through the whole of the trial.

It seemed strange, even embarrassing at times, that outside the courtroom, during coffee breaks or lunch breaks, we would sometimes see Mary, her mother Gwen and others who we had known for several years and been on friendly terms with, but could not speak to them. Because they were witnesses for the prosecution, we were told to ignore them, and no doubt they had the same instructions regarding us. A polite 'Good morning' was about all that passed between us.

Each day, Andy sat in the huge wooden dock, accompanied by a court security officer. I sat on a bench immediately next to the dock with other members of the family. The lawyers sat in front of the dock, to their left the jury, to their right the press, behind the dock was the public gallery, which was full every day, and everyone was facing the judge.

From the very beginning, when the usher called out 'All rise!' and Mrs Justice Anne Rafferty walked into her court, it was very clear that she 'ruled over her domain'. Evidently in her mid-fifties but looking younger, she was a most imposing figure in her fine scarlet robes and wig and I noticed she was carrying the black cap. When she spoke, from her manner and demeanour, she portrayed an air of obvious firmness but with understanding and fairness – and she displayed those professional qualities a great many times over the forthcoming days and weeks.

The charge of murder was put to Andy and he pleaded not guilty.

I have spent many hours in courtrooms both presenting and giving evidence, in my capacity as a police officer, but here I was watching and listening to my son – my own flesh and blood – defending himself on a charge of murdering his son, his flesh and blood, and with the prospect going to prison for life. It is not easy to explain all my emotions during the trial. At times the whole scenario seemed unreal to me, as if it was all happening to someone else, even though it was my son in the dock. My feelings changed from day to day, as new witnesses gave evidence and new facts emerged. It was difficult at times not to be overwhelmed by anger, frustration, despair and sorrow. However, the support of my family, Andy's excellent legal team, the press and the court staff, helped greatly. There were good days, we did manage to laugh at times and Andy's strength of character shone through. I have always been a positive person and my glass is always half full, never half empty. I tried to view the trial as an 'outsider looking in'. That helped me and, in truth, I also found the experience interesting and compelling. However, on many occasions, the reality of the situation came to the fore and tears would come to my eyes.

The jury, consisting of nine women and three men, was sworn in and my son's trial began. It is only natural that anyone involved in jury trials tries to 'read' the jury members and look for any slight indication or reaction they might give as they listen to the evidence. I was no different throughout the trial, despite the fact that I know from experience that it is impossible to confidently predict if a jury will find in favour of the prosecution or the accused. Any lawyer will tell you that if you could bet on jury verdicts you would undoubtedly lose money. The majority of the jury appeared middle-aged, with few younger members, and I assumed that most of them were probably married with families, but I could have been wrong.

As in all trials, on most days a great deal of legal argument and submission was presented to the judge in the absence of the jury and Mrs Justice Rafferty gave her ruling, based on the law. It had been apparent to both sides from the commencement of the case that because of the deterioration of Andy and Mary's relationship there was a danger that parts of the trial could develop into a matrimonial court, and neither party wanted that. Thus, as is usual in similar cases, 'deals' were agreed between both sides – this meant certain points or facts would be omitted by prosecution and defence if it was felt they would be irrelevant to the case being tried. Unfortunately the prosecution evidence given by some witnesses did not always follow the 'deal agreement' and as a result the defence lawyers had to obtain further evidence to refute the allegations at very short notice. An example of this was the statement that Andy had been dismissed from the army for 'bullying', which was totally untrue. Nevertheless, extra work had to be put in by Andy's lawyers to obtain his full army record and a statement from a senior officer in his regiment to prove that he left with an exemplary record.

It is not my intention to record here all the details of the trial which took place over a period of three weeks – full accounts appeared in every national newspaper and were reported by many radio and television channels – however, I do feel it important to give account of a large part of it, particularly Andy's evidence where it related to Jacob's death and the reasons for his actions. All quotations are taken from the court transcript and official tape recordings and are given with the kind permission of Marten Walsh Cherer Ltd.

Mr Katz outlined the case for the prosecution. The basis of this was that Andy was guilty of killing Jacob as an act of murder and not manslaughter. It was emphasized that under English law there is no such thing as a 'mercy killing' – it is murder. Mr Katz said that Jacob's death was a selfish act committed by Andy after a day of drinking. He told the jury that 'It is true Jacob was suffering from a terrible degenerative disease – his limited future would have been painful and distressing for himself and everyone else. But at the time of his death he was not terminally ill in the sense of being at death's door.'

The first witnesses for the prosecution were mainly medical experts and the police who dealt with Andy and Mary at the time of their arrest. Dr Ed Wraith, Consultant Paediatrician from Manchester Children's Hospital, the leading expert on mucopolysaccharidosis diseases, who had dealt with Jacob from the time he was diagnosed, explained to the jury exactly what Hunter Syndrome is, how it affects boys and not girls and what the prognosis for sufferers generally is. He said that 'Towards the end, the child would be in a vegetative state and would be doubly incontinent. Every acquired skill that child has had would be lost. That includes walking, talking and feeding.'

Dr Wraith went on to explain that Jacob suffered from the more severe form of Hunter Syndrome. He had twice recovered from pneumonia and his parents had signed an agreement allowing him to die if his breathing stopped while at a hospice. Dr Wraith also pointed out that over a period of ten years, only forty-seven babies were born with

Hunter Syndrome in the UK.

When asked by Michael Sayers, in cross-examination, if Jacob's quality of life would be: 'No quality at all,' Dr Wraith replied. 'At the very end I would agree with that statement. By the end there would be good days and bad days but as the child gets older there would be more bad days than good days.' He also agreed with Mr Sayers that a sufferer would end up deaf, dumb, hardly able to breathe and with pain and stiffness in his joints, limbs and face and possibly loss of sight.

Several witnesses who knew Jacob, having looked after him at Naomi House Hospice, Chestnut Tree House Hospice and at his schools, gave evidence and, in general, said that although Jacob was very ill his quality of life was quite good and they particularly spoke of Andy and Mary's love of their son.

One carer stated that Jacob enjoyed playing football, but when cross-examined by Mr Sayers they agreed that 'playing football' was no more than kicking a ball two or three times, not playing football as a normal ten-year-old boy would do. It was not possible to measure what Jacob did against other children at the hospice because many of them were very disabled – both physically and mentally. To the carer, kicking a ball was interpreted as 'playing football'.

Mary's mother, Mrs Gwen Richards, gave evidence. She said that Andy and Mary were two very strong-willed people and their marriage had been volatile from the start. She confirmed that Jacob's health had deteriorated rapidly in the two months prior to his death. His symptoms were more pronounced, his face had become heavy round the jaw and his stomach was bigger. She continued, 'His hands were like claws and he was unable to hold anything. He could not stretch his hands. He could only totter round at home on the tips of his toes. The rest of the time he was in a wheelchair. He had times when he would sit on the floor and shout when you tried to get him into his wheelchair if he did not want to get in it. His hearing had gone.' Despite operations, she said, Jacob would probably have died.

When cross-examined, Mrs Richards admitted that she told police in an interview, on being told of her grandson's death, 'To be honest, to hear this was the best possible news I could have had.'

Mary was in the witness box over a period of three days. She recalled her life with Andy and the eventual breakdown of their marriage, her battles with the social services, the stress of coping with Jacob, watching him regress and then the explicit detail of his death.

As with all witnesses, the Judge invited Mary to sit while giving evidence, which she did when obviously upset or stressed. She held a photograph of Jacob and also one of his dummies – she also wore a lock of his hair on her jacket. Mary was later criticized for this by Mr Sayers when, in his summing up, he suggested that Mary's 'props' were for effect. It was certainly dramatic and the press reported on it; however I am sure that the mementoes helped Mary during her court ordeal and she was entitled to do whatever she wished.

Mary gave evidence on her life with Andy, reiterating what her mother had told the court about their marriage being volatile from the start. She told of having several miscarriages prior to the shock of Jacob being born with Hunter Syndrome, and of the dreadful experience of having Henry terminated in the womb after being told that he had MPS.

Mary's demeanour was as one would have expected of a mother who had lost her son while also having to give evidence against her ex-husband. She broke down and cried a number of times, she shouted and attempted to argue when under cross-examination, and although shown sympathy by the Judge, she was rebuked by her several times. I do not know if her reactions were as a result of the strong and direct questioning of Mr Sayers, but I felt it appeared that the prosecution legal team might have advised her better as to how to give evidence – or perhaps they did and she was unable to act on their advice.

Mary testified that on the day Jacob died Andy had gone out for a drink with friends, come home briefly to see Jacob and then gone out again. During the evening, she said Andy spoke to her on the phone and sent text messages indicating that he felt Jacob was suffering, at the end of his life, and that the time had come to end his suffering. She agreed that she had discussed Jacob's condition with Andy. She said she was not sure if he meant it or not but did admit saying to him 'What are we waiting for?' Mary explained to the jury that she meant 'What are we waiting for in life, what does the future hold for us?'

She denied throughout that she knew what Andy intended to do, or that she had anything to do with Jacob's death.

She said that she left the house at about 11 p.m., with George, after receiving text messages and phone calls from Andy asking her to take their son to her mother's in order, she believed, that they might enjoy a night of sex. Mary also admitted that after leaving the house she visited a late-night garage, where she purchased a drink and crisps for George and a bottle of wine. Having already drunk wine at home earlier, she sat in a quite road and drank some of the wine she had purchased. When she received the phone call from Andy informing her that Jacob was dead, she took George to her mother's and then returned to her own house.

Mary told the court that on arriving home she found Andy kneeling next to Jacob's bed cuddling his lifeless body. She told Andy not to phone the police immediately but to have a glass of wine with her and drink a toast to their son. Andy had been drinking, she said, but was not drunk.

She admitted that when the police and paramedics arrived and they attempted to resuscitate Jacob she became hysterical and tried to stop them. Because of her behaviour at that time she was arrested and taken into custody, suspected of being involved in Jacob's death. She was later released without charge.

The next part of the prosecution evidence was very dramatic, revealing and heartbreaking. The recording of Andy's emergency call was played. Actually, it was played several times during the trial and it never became easier to listen to. The first time I heard it I cried silently – and it was very noticeable that several members of the jury reacted in the same way.

The court was hushed as Andy's voice echoed loudly across the room. In the dock, his head was bowed and he stared at the floor as the recording was played.

'I have murdered my son. I killed him.' Andy said to the emergency operator.

'How?' he was asked.

'With a pillow over the face,' Andy replied. Asked why he had done it, he said, 'I don't want to comment any more. That's all you need to know.' Andy confirmed that his wife was in the house with him and that she was perfectly all right and safe.

It is poignant to note that, apart from that conversation, Andy has never used the word 'murder' – he always believed his ending of Jacob's life was not murder but an act of mercy.

Police officers then gave evidence of their attendance at the house, one testifying that on entering he was met by Andy who said, 'I have terminated my son's life, so arrest me.'

En route to the police station Andy said, 'Please don't judge me before you know the facts. It was a mercy killing. My son wanted me to do it because he was terminally ill. I loved my son so much. Now I have to stand up in court and say I put a pillow over his head.'

The next witnesses to testify were two pathologists who carried out post mortems on Jacob. They did not appear in person and their statements were read out to the jury and not challenged by the defence. They both confirmed that Jacob was, in their opinion, suffering from advanced stages of Hunter Syndrome and approaching the end of his life. They gave medical evidence of their autopsies and the results of the toxicology tests that were carried out. But the most important and vital evidence given by both pathologists was that, had they not known that Andy had admitted suffocating Jacob, because of the poor condition of his airways, which were partially blocked, they would have readily signed a death certificate confirming that Jacob had died as a consequence of the effects of mucopolysaccharidosis – Hunter Syndrome.

The implication of this testimony was that had Andy telephoned the family doctor, who had known and treated Jacob for most of the time he lived in Worthing, instead of contacting the police, then it is likely that a death certificate would have been signed and Andy would not have been charged with causing his death. As a family, we have often discussed this scenario. If Andy had not telephoned the police and 'confessed' to what he had done, things, both for him and for us, the wider family, would have been very different. But Andy says that he always wanted to, and always has, told the truth about why he ended his son's suffering – he could not have lived a lie for the rest of his life. I so admire him for that.

I actually know of a parent, who, many years ago, ended the life of their terminally ill child in order to bring its suffering to an end, but did not tell their spouse, who remains even to this day unaware of it. How hard it must be to go through life unable to share that secret with anyone.

Dealing with the allegation that Andy was drunk when he killed his son, it was agreed by the police that when he was arrested Andy had been drinking but was not drunk – which Mary agreed with. The prosecution produced a written statement from a so-called 'expert witness' in which he said he scientifically worked out that at the time Andy smothered Jacob he was very drunk and probably hardly able to stand up. That evidence was totally refuted by Dr Wright when he testified, who basically said that although Andy had consumed a large amount of alcohol during the day and evening, because of the fact that (a) he was used to regular drinking and (b) his state of tension etc. in anticipation of what he was going to do, then the chemical reactions in his body could change and render him to a state of being fairly sober and far from very drunk.

Several other minor witnesses testified for the prosecution, were cross-examined by Mr Sayers and, after, approximately eight days, Mr Katz closed their case.

ABOVE: The Wragg Family: (back row,l to r) Tina, Steve and Andy; (front row, l to r) Bob, Anne and Chris.

RIGHT: Andy with his proud Mum, Anne, at the Royal Signals Regiment pass-off parade, Catterick, October 1992.

ABOVE: My first grandchild, Jacob, when he was just a few days old. Notice the Southampton mug - brainwashing at such an early age?

LEFT: Jacob with Andy on his return from Bosnia in 1994.

BELOW: They recruit them young these days!

ABOVE: Mary with Jacob at his christening in Worthing. The Rev Jimmy Morrison (right), Army Chaplain, conducted the service.

BELOW: Enjoying a candlelit dinner with Anne.

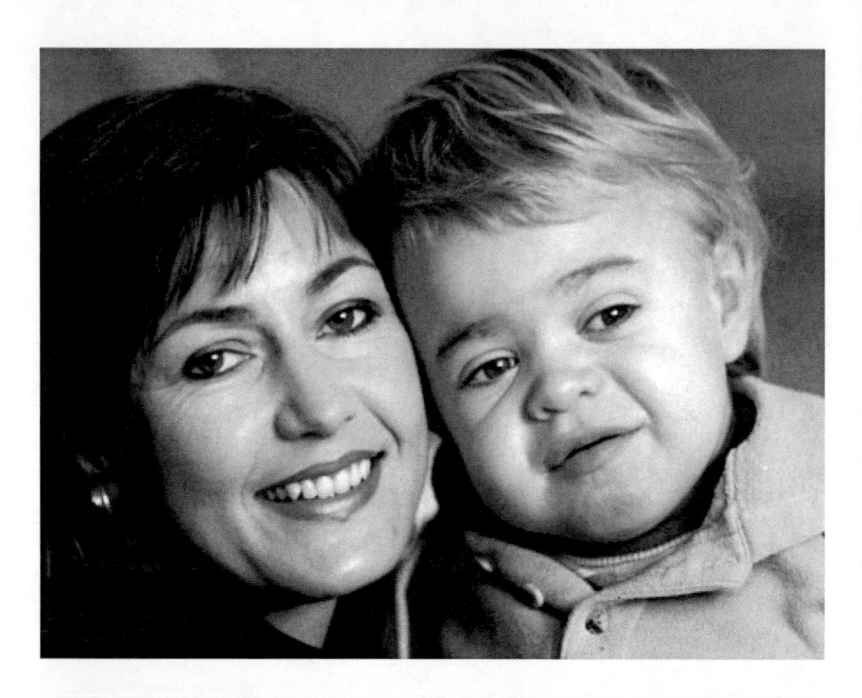

LEFT: Mary and Jacob, aged three years.

BELOW LEFT: Happy days with Anne in our garden in Worthing.

RIGHT: Jacob was heartbroken when his precious pedal car was stolen, but it was replaced shortly afterwards by an anonymous donor.

BELOW: Jacob and Grandad enjoying happy days in Hereford, 1996.

ABOVE: Jacob always loved the water. Here he is on holiday in Florida, testing the water for himself (above right) and, with his mum and dad, watching his favourite character 'Free Willy' perform for the crowds.

LEFT: 'Big hugs!' Jacob with his beloved Free Willy toy in his garden in Worthing.

ABOVE RIGHT: With Uncle Ray in the helicopter at the Royal Naval Air Station, Culdrose, Cornwall, 1988.

RIGHT: With his cousins Garry, Kelly and Holly.

TOP: 'The Boys'. Uncle Chris, Grandad Bob, Jacob and Daddy. Chris and Jacob are wearing the Southampton football kit – prior to Jacob supporting Chelsea.

BELOW: Jacob aged five or six. Anne and I love this photograph.

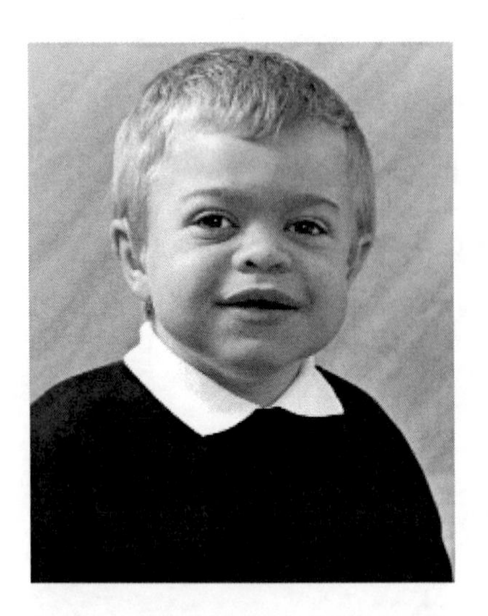

RIGHT: Still a Southampton supporter … Practicing for the next 'big gig'.

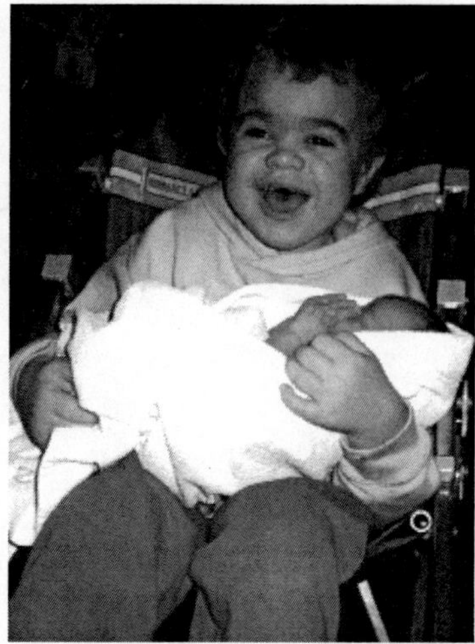

ABOVE: And then there were two! A delighted Grandad with Jacob and newborn George.

ABOVE RIGHT: 'This is my new brother!'

RIGHT: Mary and the boys enjoying one of the many lovely walks in Hereford.

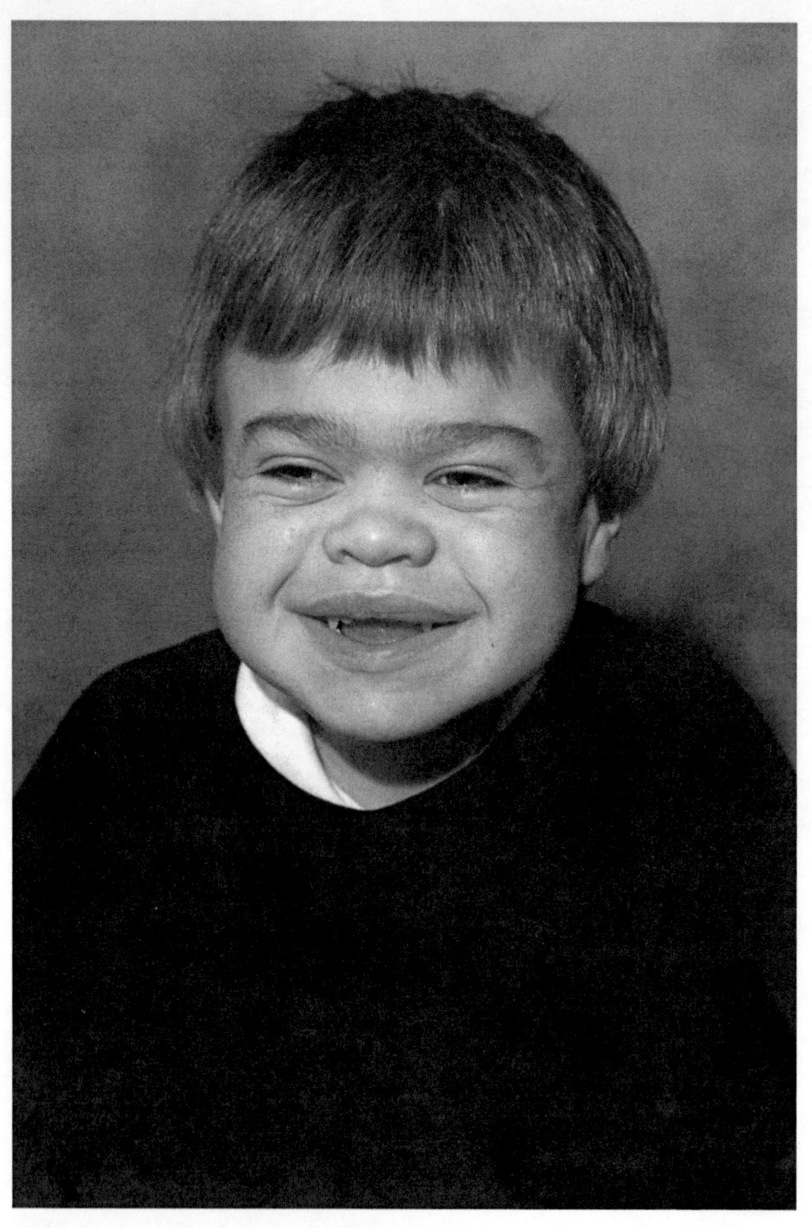

ABOVE: Jacob aged seven years in his school uniform.

ABOVE: Jacob with Santa at Goring Hall, the hospital where Anne has worked for many years.

RIGHT: Luckily Jacob was wearing his Chelsea shirt the day he met Chelsea and France footballer Frank LeBoeuf at Gatwick Airport!

ABOVE: In goal for Manchester United, with faithful dog Charlie in the background.

LEFT: Jamie Oliver eat your heart out!

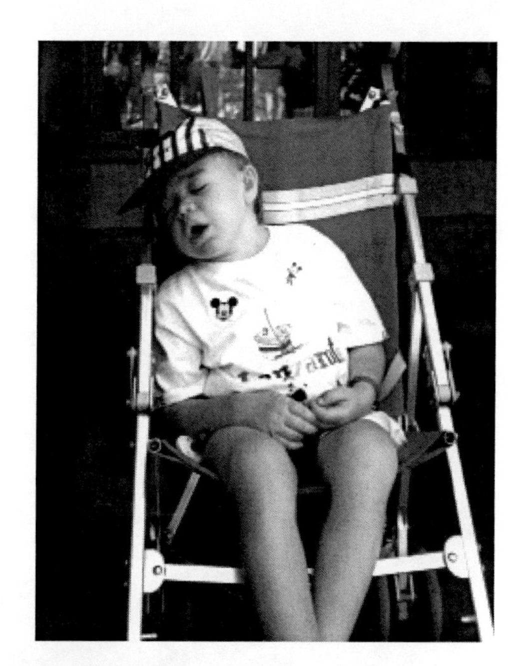

RIGHT: 'My busy day …!'

BELOW: Grandad getting some practice with the guitar.

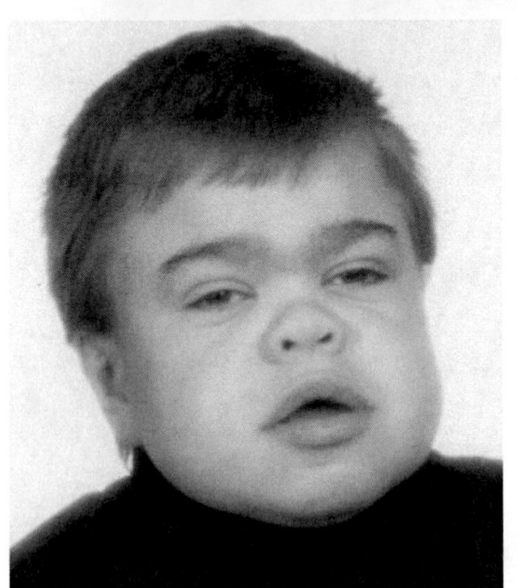

ABOVE: Jacob aged about nine. Never too old to sit on Grandad's knee.

LEFT: Jacob aged nine.

RIGHT: The order of service for Jacob's remembrance celebration at Chestnut Tree House.

In loving memory of
Jacob Henry Wragg
23-11-93
A service of remembrance & celebration
Monday 16th August 2004
At The Chestnut
Tree Childrens Hospice 10.30- 2.30

LEFT: With Andy at the MPS Society's Children's Wood in Sherwood Forest, Nottinghamshire, 2006.

BELOW: Andy planting an oak sapling in memory of Jacob.

Chapter 8

The First Trial: The Case for the Defence

At the end of each day's hearing, Andy attended conferences with his lawyers, and the rest of the family returned to Worthing. We would have our meal, sometimes going out to a restaurant, and then spend many hours discussing the day's court proceedings and trying to evaluate the evidence and how it would be interpreted by the jury. Some nights I slept well, but quite often Anne and I would be up at three or four in the morning drinking tea, unable to sleep. During the two weekends of the trial, we tried to occupy ourselves taking the dog for long walks or just trying to relax and 'charge our batteries' ready for the following week.

Although I was quite positive at that stage of the trial, we all remained realistic. We, and above all Andy, knew that a life sentence was still a real possibility for which we had to be prepared.

Before the trial, Andy's lawyers were contacted by at least two families who had Hunter boys, both of whom offered to give evidence in Andy's defence. They knew how stressful and difficult it was to cope and they also said that they understood Andy's action – a statement was obtained from one of the parents and the offer was very much appreciated. However, a decision was made by Mr Sayers not to use that evidence on the basis that for every parent who gave such testimony, there could be another who had opposite views, every case should be judged on its individual facts.

The case for the defence commenced on Wednesday 9 March 2005. Anne and the other defence witnesses waiting to testify waited outside but the court was packed with press and members of the public as Andy, wearing a dark suit, white shirt and blue tie entered the witness box and clearly took the oath. Andy was in the witness box over two days.

The atmosphere was highly charged. In order to set the scene, it is my intention to give the reader a fair and balanced account from the trial transcripts of the proceedings and in particular the testimony Andy gave, both in his evidence-in-chief and cross-examination, but omitting parts which are less important or irrelevant. The transcripts record far better than I can the true emotions and feelings Andy had when he ended his beloved son's life. QS indicates a question put by Defence Counsel, Mr Michael Sayers, QC; A indicates an answer given by Andy; QK indicates a question put by Prosecution Counsel, Mr Philip Katz, QC. JR is Mrs Justice Rafferty.

In the first part of Andy's evidence, in response to Mr Sayers's questions, he confirmed his personal details, related relevant parts of his family history; confirmed that when he was two his eight-month-old baby sister had died of pneumonia; gave details of his education and employment history. He then testified about meeting Mary; getting married; joining the Army; Jacob's birth in November 1993; and Mary becoming pregnant with Henry.

QS Can you tell us please, in your own words, how did you learn first that Jacob was diagnosed with Hunter's Syndrome?

A A few weeks before, um, we thought there may be a problem with Jacob . . . I was in Harrogate . . ./ I was aware that Jacob was having tests . . . Whilst I was in the lectures she [Mary] rang me from Hereford, um, and said, 'He's dying. He's dying' . . . she couldn't express any more than that, and couldn't really tell me how, why or what, you know, what he was dying of . . . I was on a train within an hour, on my way back to Hereford, to see Mary. At that time they'd arranged another appointment the following morning to give us more details on what the diagnosis and prognosis was for him . . . The following morning the three of us went down to the hospital to see a paediatrician who gave us [pause] the news of what the disorder was. He knew it was an MPS disorder but at that stage he didn't know which strain or which type of MPS disorder it was, er – and actually told us stuff that wasn't actually true that might happen to Jacob. Um, and at that stage I don't think either of us actually realized the implications for Henry, the unborn child, but at the end of that meeting they did bring it to our attention that we needed to test Henry, the unborn baby.

QS Mary told us that the diagnosis of Jacob evolved over two or three days, that was her evidence, I am paraphrasing it. Is that right?

A Yes.

QS And was a decision taken to examine the unborn child to see whether or not he carried the same problem?

A Yes, sir, we discussed it at length.

QS And she told us that there was an amniocentesis set up for the child to be examined?

A That's correct.

QS In two or three days' time?

A That's correct.

QS And that took place?

A Uh-huh.

QS And then you had to wait, of course, for that particular investigation, for five days before you got a result?

A Yes, sir.

QS Just in parenthesis, during those five days was it just you, Mary and Jacob?

A No. Mary's parents came down, as well as my parents and my brother Steve came down . . .

QS Sadly, the result of the amniocentesis on the unborn child, who you later called 'Henry', proved positive?

A Yes.

QS I don't think there is any dispute about it, but Mary told us that the unborn baby was seven or seven and a half months?

A That's correct.

QS What happened?

A We discussed what we would do if the results came back that Henry was a carrier of the disease; and under advice from paediatricians and professionals we trusted to know what they were talking about, said that we really didn't want to bring another Hunter into the world because of the terrible things that happen to them, so we decided that when we went for the results of the amnio that if it was bad news, we would terminate, and we would terminate as and when they decided was best, because they said it would happen quite quickly after the test results came in. Um . . .

QS Right. That was obviously very late in the pregnancy. And was this a decision made . . . well, who made the decision?

A Me and Mary made the decision under the advice of doctors.

QS Was anybody disapproving of that decision . . .

A No, sir.

QS . . . to terminate . . .

A No, sir.

QS . . . the pregnancy at seven and a half months?

A No.

QS I then have to ask you about the actual termination.

A Uh-huh.

QS Mary told us that you were given two hours to make this decision . . .

A That's correct.

QS . . . as to terminate it or not. Is that correct?

A That's correct.

QS As soon as you, with the doctors, had made that decision, what happened?

A Um, we didn't even go back to the house, Mary stayed at the hospital, we had the stuff – we had the overnight bags with us just in case we were going straight to terminating which is exactly what happened. I was, er, taken aside. Me and Mary discussed whether I wanted to be there, and whether she wanted me there, and I decided I would be there for her.

QS And did she want you there?

A Yes. The doctor that was performing the termination, er, had told me that it was the first time the hospital had carried out the procedure, um, and would I want to – did I want to be there, and I said I did. At that stage he didn't explain what the procedure was, he just said 'You can be'.

QS Did you have any idea what the procedure involved?

A No, sir.

QS Did there come a time when the procedure was ready to go ahead?

A Yes.

QS Was that that same day?

A Yes.

QS Tell us about it?

A Um, it was, er, I wouldn't say it was an operating theatre, it was just a small room where I would think they do scans for babies. Um, Mary was, er, taken in with me, heavily sedated.

QS Sorry? You were heavily sedated, or Mary?

A Mary was sedated, I wasn't, er, taking anything. Um, I went into the room. Just by Mary's head they put a stool behind me and said, er, 'If at any time you feel faint just sit down', um . . . and . . .

QS You were standing?

A Yes. Which is when I started wondering what was going to happen. But, anyway, the next thing I know they got a coin . . .

QS Sorry to interrupt. You say you were standing by her head, were you touching her at all?

A I was holding her hand, I believe.

QS Yes. What sort of equipment was in the room?

A There was an ultrasound scanner, um, apart from that there was just medical instruments which they were going to use for the procedure. Um . . .

QS Was the ultrasound activated?

A It was, and it was behind Mary's head, but it was next to me so I could see it.

QS And what did you see?

A They scanned Mary – or they scanned Henry for his heart, um, on the ultrasound . . .

(At this point in his evidence the courtroom was absolutely silent apart from Andy's voice which was quiet but audible. He frequently paused whilst reliving this horrific account. He was obviously very emotional but controlled.)

A . . . Once they'd seen . . . or once they'd found his heart beating, they found the heart, er, they placed a coin on Mary's tummy and pressed it to get a mark. I guess to – to, place the needle, er, a two-foot long needle, straight into Mary's stomach, into the baby, um, stabbing around trying to find the heart, um, which they eventually did. [Pause. Andy stood with his head bowed and eyes closed for about a minute, and then continued]. Um, and then two doctors discussed how much fluid, whatever it was they were injecting into his heart, they would need to stop the heart beating, and they needed two attempts, they needed to put a second lot in because the heart was still beating, and then they said, er, 'It's finished, it's gone' meaning the heartbeat had gone, and that was Henry terminated.

QS And you saw all that on the screen?

A Yes, sir.

QS Could you see when the heart of the unborn child ceased to beat?

A Yes.

QS After the termination of the unborn child, what happened?

A Within half an hour Mary was taken up to the maternity ward at Hereford, and labour was induced; and approximately eight hours later Henry was born, obviously dead.

QS Now you said that Mary was sedated; could she see what was going on on the screen?

A No

QS But you could?

A Yes, sir.

QS What effect did that have on you?

A Um [pause], it was horrific. I couldn't understand why they didn't tell me what was going to happen. I had no idea what was going to happen. I didn't know how they were going to do this, and, um, and I think if I'd've known I think I probably wouldn't have chosen to be there.

QS Is it a memory that you are easily able to discard?

A [Pause] It's very vivid. If I ever think about it I remember, I remember it very well, but, yeah, I try to not [pause] think about it.

As I sat looking across the courtroom at my son Andy telling this dreadful story, I realized he was describing the death of our unborn grandson. Mary was sitting listening in tears; on reflection, I suppose that was the first time she had heard in graphic detail what had happened to her and how her unborn son's life had been terminated – one can't imagine the heartache she must have been experiencing at that moment. It was plainly obvious that Andy's testimony had affected many who heard it – I noticed several of the jury and press, some hardened journalists, in tears.

The next part of the evidence was Andy confirming details of his army career. It was quite lengthy and virtually all his official records and reports were produced, mainly to refute the untrue allegations made by the prosecution that he had been dismissed from the service because of bullying. He had been disciplined for failing to sign out and in from his barracks.

QS Were you ever disciplined in the SAS for bullying anybody?

A Never, sir. I am not a bully, I never have been, and that was completely untrue.

Mr Sayers read to the jury many reports on Andy from his senior officers, all highly complimentary and recommending him for promotion, which he attained. One report stated. 'Signaller Wragg is an extremely mature, ambitious soldier who radiates self-confidence and over this last reporting period demonstrated without question the qualities that make him stand out above his peers.' It was confirmed that Andy's discharge papers from the army described his conduct as 'exemplary'.

Andy was then asked about the period after he had left the army, when he and Mary moved to Worthing and about the time he left Mary for a period of about three years.

QS Can you tell us? How did that come about? And what were the relations between you leading up to that separation?

A At that time the strain on the marriage was huge, um, Jacob was becoming more and more reliant on us, on Mary, for his care. The marriage wasn't going well . . . and I made a conscious decision that I would make a real effort for a month just to see how things went; but as far as I was concerned George was around, he was coming up to two years old and he was involved in the arguing, or he was seeing the arguing, and I didn't want him to see that, so I decided that I would make a real effort for a month and at the end of that I would make a decision as to whether the marriage was going to work or not. And I was conscious of the fact that because George was two – obviously Jacob wasn't an issue because of his limiting lifespan – but I thought I wanted to, if I was going to finish the marriage I needed to do it while George was young enough to cope with it; I felt if he got any older it would affect him more.

QS And did you leave the home?

A Yes, sir, I did.

QS We have heard talk, both from you and from Mary, of you taking Jacob swimming . . . at the weekends when you were coming home from Kettering. When you moved to Worthing did you continue that habit?

A Yes, sir, um, it was something that me and Jacob did generally. It was only me and Jacob, Mary would normally, you know, have a lie-in or do whatever she wanted to do, and it was a thing that me and Jacob did together. Um, that stopped when I left Mary. The following week I rang her and said, 'Can I pick Jacob up as normal to take him swimming?' and she refused to let me take him.

Andy then testified that Mary had prevented him from seeing Jacob, and although his GP had recommended swimming was good for the boy, he was unable to take him.

QS In the times that you did take Jacob swimming, were you ever embarrassed by his condition?

A No, never, that's, um, that's probably one of the worse things I've heard this week. I was proud of my son.

Andy went on to tell the jury that because of his difficulty in being allowed to see his sons he went to a family court three times to obtain an access order but it was not always adhered to.

He also said that during his three-year separation he lived with two other women, which Mary knew about.

QS And over the three years that you were separated, did you see Mary and the children?

A Um, it was difficult because the courts – having to go through the courts, it takes time, and I wasn't seeing as much of the boys as I wanted – as I would have liked – but it wasn't through lack of trying, it was because Mary wouldn't let me.

QS Did there come a time when you got back together with Mary?

A There did.

QS Tell us how that came about?

A I met – I went with Mary to, um, a Harvest Festival Service for George at his school, and we chatted, we seemed to be getting on better, we both seemed to have calmed down slightly, and that led to me, er, not just taking the boys away but spending some time at the bungalow with Mary and the boys, and that led to her inviting me round to dinner, then we would get the odd babysitter and we would go out together, and that led to me eventually deciding to try again.

QS And did you move back into Henty Close with her?

A Yes, sir.

The next part of the evidence covered the period when Andy had his own business, a video rental shop, and he explained that because it was losing money he decided to sell it and try to find employment in the security business. He described the close-protection and weapons course he completed in Spain, prior to being offered a position with a security company in Iraq.

QS Did you get a job working in Iraq?

A Er, yes, immediately I finished the close-protection course I was offered work by the company I later worked for in Iraq.

QS Would you tell us a bit about that, please? Working in Iraq, what exactly was your job in the close-protection work? And where were you? And what did you have to do? What was it like working in Baghdad?

A Um, I was based in Baghdad all but two weeks, my last two weeks I spent in Kurdistan, which is a lot safer than Baghdad, but predominantly I was based in Baghdad. Our job was to escort predominantly Americans who were restructuring the financial side of Iraq, to the different ministries, banks, um, wherever they wanted to go, basically downtown in Baghdad, working in four-man teams, two in each vehicle, with the client in the lead vehicle with the commanding officer, if you like; sometimes in armoured vehicles, sometimes not in armoured vehicles.

QS And how were you protected?

A Um, if we were involved in . . .

QS With what?

A Oh, sorry. We carried AK47s.

QS AK47 is a rifle, is it?

A It is, yes. Russian.

QS Yes?

A And smoke, we had quite a lot of smoke grenades, and grenades and stuff like that.

QS And what was it like in doing this job in Baghdad?

A Um, we were actually located in the green zone when we weren't working, er, and that is probably the safest place in Bagdad, although it is mortared regularly. Um, and outside the green zone is pretty terrifying. Your . . . you were constantly at threat of death.

QS And this is where you took people from the green zone to the various places?

A Yes.

QS Did you experience any difficulties in doing your job?

A Yes, we had a few, er, it had its moments. The closest . . . I mean, there were explosions every day, people were killed every day and are killed every day. The closest I came, er, to a suicide bomb on the 14th July Bridge, which is just outside the green zone. I'd picked up the Iraqi drivers, which was my job that morning, to pick them up at a roundabout by the bridge. I picked them up and, um, I just walked back into the office room, which was the other side of the Tigris, and a suicide bomber blew himself up, along with a few Americans and some Iraqis, er, and it . . . it blew the windows out, we hit the floor, we thought we'd come under attack but then realized quite soon it was a suicide bomb. It was too big to be a mortar. Two friends that were in my, um, chalet if you like, where we were accommodated, were shot one in the back one in the back of the head . . . Um, three or four guys from other companies died while I was there, and since I've got back I've lost one good friend and two colleagues who have been shot and killed . . . well, two were blown up by a suicide bomb.

QS And how did this seemingly dangerous life affect you?

A Well, at the time, um, I just got on with it, to be honest, it was, er, a question of just getting your head down and getting through it and getting on with it, and just doing what you can to try and alleviate the – the threat.

QS During the time that you were in Iraq, was there any communication between yourself and Mary?

A I would speak to Mary most days, or text most days . . . I would speak to George most days as well.

QS Were you able to speak to Jacob?

A No he – Mary would pass messages to him, and stuff like that, but, no, he wasn't able to communicate.

QS This was the beginning of 2004, was he able to hear?

A No, he was profoundly deaf.

QS How much were you hoping to earn in this occupation?

A Well, it was, er . . . it was in the region of £80,000, tax free, for a year's work.

QS And had you completed your year's work, would that have resolved your financial situation?

A Yes, sir.

QS On 9 July your term of service ended and you had a leave period and you returned to this country?

A Yes, sir.

QS Did you go straight home?

A No, sir.

QS Where did you go?

A I spent the night in London with the guys that we'd – that I'd flown back with, er, because Baghdad and Iraq is not somewhere where you drink, it's not advisable, and we didn't do it, it wasn't, er, it wouldn't have been good for people to be drinking at night.

QS When did you go home?

A The following morning.

QS When you got home, was Jacob there?

A No, Mary was out with the boys, I believe.

QS Was he living at home?

A He was, yes.

QS He was living at home, and George. Mary told us that you went to Center Parcs for I think it was four or five days?

A That's correct.

QS Who was that with?

A With George. We dropped Jacob off at Naomi House, the Children's Hospice, on the way to Center Parcs.

QS And how did you find Jacob on your return? You had been away for how long? Two, three months?

A Nearly three months. Um, I also hadn't seen him for quite a bit before that because I'd been on a course for about a month, so it was, yes, three, just over three months I would say. And, um, yes, he was, er . . .

QS I am sorry, you had been in Iraq for just over three months?

A Yes.

QS Plus the month before when you had been on a course . . . so you had not actually seen him for about four months. Is that right?

A No, I had seen him very briefly between going to Iraq, but not for any length of time.

QS Did you find any changes in him?

A There was massive changes in him. He was, er, he was completely different, er, he was . . . I don't think he recognized me at all. He was so much more lethargic than he was before I left. Um, he had lost – I believe all communication had gone.

QS Could he speak at all?

A No. His, er, face – his head had changed, his face had changed, the . . .

QS I am sorry. You say his head and face were changed. In what way?

A Well, it had become more deformed, his skull was more deformed than it had been, um, and you could tell that by feeling his head, and he had a lot of hair, but, um, he'd also, we believe, had a stroke two years previous when he had pneumonia in Worthing, we believed he'd had a stroke and his face was drooping down one side, and that was more prominent when I got back as well.

QS You say two years before, is that the occasion which Mary told us about when he nearly died?

A Yes, sir, yes.

QS When he was eight. What about his hands?

A His hands were more clawed, um, his – his . . .

QS For the record, you are demonstrating with your own hands, the fingers are curled?

A Yes.

QS Was he able to . . .

A He couldn't, um, do more than that [indicating] I would say.

QS You are just opening your fingers a little bit?

A Yes, he couldn't open . . .

QS We have a photograph of him holding a video?

A Yes, he would with two hands, or he could just about hold it with one or . . .

QS Before you went to Iraq was he able to put a video on himself?

A No, he could – he could just about get it in the machine but he couldn't actually, um, put it on unless the machine was that type where it would automatically start itself, but as far as, you know, working the machine itself, no, no, he couldn't.

QS And what about his feet? Any changes there?

A Well, he was, you know, completely on tiptoes, um, and he didn't seem to be as mobile – half as mobile – as he used to be . . . normally you would see him running or tiptoeing around the house, and that seemed to have gone, he was in his room most of the time.

QS We have heard suggestions that he was playing football. What do you have to say about that?

A Er, he could never play football, and towards the end if he could – he would go toward a ball and kick it, and he would kick it twice and then go back in the house. He'd never played football. I mean, it's . . .

QS When he kicked the ball once or twice was he still on tiptoes? Or was he . . .

A Yes, completely. And it could have been a fence or a door, it could have been anything, but not particularly – I would not say he could play football.

QS So whilst he could hit a ball with his tiptoe'd foot, you would not regard that as playing football?

A No, I would not, sir.

QS Anything else about Jacob at this time before you go off to Center Parcs?

A No. As I say, just the fact that he was getting very, very tired later on in the day, which was, um, wasn't the case before I left, he seemed to have a lot more energy before I left.

QS You say you didn't think he recognized you?

A No.

QS . . . When you returned from Center Parcs Jacob was still at

Naomi House?

A That's correct.

QS . . . He was picked up on 22 July. I would like to interrupt the chronology at this point. What was your understanding of Jacob's future and the consequences of the degenerative disease that he suffered from?

A Um, well, I didn't believe that Jacob did have a future, and any future he did have was going to be, um, painful [pause] and [pause] undignified and [pause] . . .

QS What about his characteristics, the physical characteristics, the physical changes that would occur with the disease?

A The biggest problem for me was that, um, [pause] I never knew if he was in pain, I thought he was, but he could not express pain normally, and, er, I thought he was in pain and couldn't tell us, and it was getting worse rapidly.

QS We have heard that . . . at times he was laughing?

A He would laugh, yes, he would smile, but I didn't believe he was smiling for any particular reason then, I just think it was a, a muscle reaction that he was having, I – I couldn't do anything to make him laugh, he wasn't laughing at anything specific, I didn't feel.

QS At times there was this video that he watched called Free Willy?

A Yes, sir.

QS About a whale. The suggestion is that he knew it so well that he anticipated, for instance, the moment when the whale jumps out over the barrier to get out into freedom, and that delighted him?

A Yes.

QS What do you say about that? Is that accurate? Did he do that?

A I didn't see that towards the end. That film was one that me and him had watched when he was a [pause] lot younger, and it was the only film he ever sat through, with me, from start to finish. Um, and later on, er, like family videos, it was very hard for me to tell what his brain was doing as far as recognition, whether he actually understood the film he was watching.

QS When you came back from Iraq, how far could he walk?

A Well, if he didn't fall over, he could possibly get to the middle or to the back of the garden and then probably back into the house, but that would tire him.

QS How far before he would fall over?

A I would say 30 metres, 40 metres.

QS What about his wheelchair, what part did that play?

A It was his life. He was, er, whenever he left the bungalow he was in his wheelchair, and he was restrained in the wheelchair, that was the beauty of the wheelchair at times, if he was strapped in he couldn't get out and do what he wanted.

QS . . . The suggestion has been made that you favoured George, you spent more time with George than you did with Jacob. Of your two sons you spent more time with George. What do you say about that?

A That's completely untrue. Um, George and Jacob had different needs, and George could do a lot of things that Jacob couldn't even think about doing, so therefore some of the activities I did with George didn't include Jacob, but that's the way it was. Um, George – I would say that I favoured Jacob, I would always put Jacob first before George, and it used to infuriate George because if Jacob ever came in the garden and we were doing anything, I would always stop and do it with Jacob and explain to George why we were doing it with Jacob, 'Because it's not going to last, it will be a couple of minutes and then Jacob will be back in his room watching his video, but while he's here we've got to include him, he's part of the family.' It's ridiculous to suggest that I favoured him over Jacob.

QS How about his swallowing ability?

A He, um, from probably 2001, maybe even before, he would regularly choke at the dinner table and have to be – well we would have to try and get the food out of him. Several times, you know, we thought he'd gone, he would go blue and we would have to dislodge the food or the obstruction for him to be able to breathe properly.

QS And was this the same? Or had the position changed at all since you had last seen him three or four months before?

A Yes, it had changed. He was, um, he was out of breath constantly, he didn't have any – he didn't have the energy to shout any more, or, you know, the noises he did make were not loud because he obviously didn't have the lung capacity, or the blockage in his throat was so bad that he couldn't get enough air into his lungs I don't think.

QS Jacob was at Naomi House until Thursday 22nd. On Wednesday 21st there was a social services meeting at your house, 68 Henty Close . . . did you attend the social services meeting?

A No, I did not. I did go in and say 'Hello' but I didn't actually attend the meeting.

QS Why didn't you attend the meeting?

A Um, I never, um, or I say 'never', er, from a very early – early stage I became disillusioned with social services and therefore would leave any, um, anything to do with social services to Mary because I would get frustrated and angry at the false promises that they would make and then never deliver.

Andy then described how he spent time with George on Wednesday 21 July, when they both slept in a tent in the garden, with Jacob on Thursday 22 July, and how he went out with friends he hadn't seen since returning from Iraq on Friday 23 July.

QS My Lady, I was about to get to 24th July. The witness has been giving evidence for nearly an hour and three-quarters. I wonder if your Ladyship would feel a short break might be appropriate?

JR I am entirely in your hands, Mr Sayers. If Mr Wragg would profit from a fifteen-minute break then we shall have one . . . Yes, ladies and gentlemen, have a brief break and come back to us for five to twelve. Mr Wragg, leave the witness box and don't discuss your evidence with anyone.

A No, my Lady.

The court adjourned. During the adjournment, Andy stayed on his own not speaking to anyone. I joined Anne, Chris and Steve, who were waiting to give evidence, for a cup of coffee. We made fairly light conversation, I told them that Andy was doing well in the witness box, but my thoughts were turning to the evidence I knew I was about to hear for the first time – how Jacob had died. I had heard Mary give her testimony of returning to the house and finding Andy with Jacob, but I was now preparing for something that I knew would have a profound effect on me. The court re-convened.

QS Just before I get to Saturday 24th July there are two matters which I would like to raise with you. When you returned from Iraq and you had been abroad did you intend going anywhere else when you came back here?

A Yes. Um, I'd talked with Mary.

QS Did you intend going anywhere else?

A A holiday you mean?

QS Yes.

A Yes.

QS Where? . . . Did you plan anything?

A Yes. Immediately we returned from Center Parcs I booked a week's holiday in Gran Canaria.

QS For whom?

A Myself, just myself.

QS Why was that? Why did you book a holiday just to go on your own?

A Two reasons. One was for tax reasons. The way my leave was planning out, that I would need to spend at least two weeks of my leave out of the country, so my plan was to spend a week of my first leave and a week of my last leave out of the country. And the second was to totally wind down and relax before my return to Baghdad.

QS How were you getting on with Mary at this stage?

A Not particularly well, although she was aware that I was going to . . . er, there was a strong possibility that I would do that. I mentioned this before I even went to Iraq . . . and said that there's a strong possibility I might need a week away on my own, just to, er, get myself together for another tour and she – she was agreeable to that.

QS She didn't mind not being taken?

A Not then. She did – when I actually booked it she did – she wasn't happy, yes.

QS The other question I want to ask you about, which I omitted to ask you about is would you go back to the Wednesday night, the night you camped in the garden with George. Did you watch television that night?

A Yes, sir. There was a documentary on, a story about a boy called Lorenzo, called *Lorenzo's Oil*, which there's also been a film about. There was a documentary about his, um, his family's life as well as his, which I watched with Mary, which was quite, um, upsetting. We tended not to watch, um, programmes about children's hospitals and stuff like that, because it was too upsetting, but on this occasion we did watch *Lorenzo's Oil*, um, and there's some big similarities with his genetic disorder.

QS Pausing there. There is a movie called *Lorenzo's Oil*?

A Correct.

QS And the documentary was about the movie or the facts behind the movie?

A It was about the facts of the family and the struggle that they had had with Lorenzo, and the basic outline is that the father and the mother became qualified doctors and made it their life's work to try and find a cure for Lorenzo, er, which they never did, but they did – they did invent a substance called Lorenzo's Oil, which did prolong life of the children with that genetic disorder for some considerable time.

QS Again, without going into detail, what effect did that have on your mind?

A I don't really know. I just remember I was quite upset watching it, particularly from the father's point of view because it had, um, it had quite an effect on him and his wife and an effect on the siblings of them, because of this condition.

QS Did you relate to the documentary in any way?

A Yes, it was, um, similar in many ways. Er, it was a debilitating disease. Lorenzo, I believe, is still alive but he's, um, in a vegetative state, er, so their life's work was not a cure, they didn't find a cure.

QS Now, I want you to go to Saturday morning, (24th July). What happened on Saturday morning? . . . Did you stay in the house or did you go out?

Andy then told the jury that on that Saturday he went shopping to buy some bits and pieces for his forthcoming holiday, which was due to start in two days' time. He then went to the TMG Club, a family social club to which he belonged. Andy had taken George there on several occasions but not Jacob as he thought it not the ideal environment for him.

He went on to say that he had a pint of lager at the club and then drove home as he had promised to look after Jacob while Mary had her nails manicured at home.

QS Who was at the bungalow when you got there?

A Jacob was in his bedroom, Mary was having her nails done.

QS And George, where was he?

A He was with his grandmother.

QS What was Jacob doing?

A Immediately, when I went into the house, he was watching a video.

QS Did you see Jacob? Did you go into his room at all?

A I did. Um, I sat down and chatted to Mary for approximately ten minutes and then went into Jacob's room and spent approximately twenty minutes to half an hour with him.

QS Right. Can you tell us, please, how was that? How did you spend that twenty minutes to half an hour with him?

A He was – he was sat on his bed watching his videos and, er, I was just kneeling in front of him talking to him.

QS Was he able to respond at all?

A No.

QS Did you do anything together, apart from him watching videos, when you were talking to him?

A Um, no, there wasn't much interaction, apart from him staring at me, er, and then me looking at him and realizing that he was in a bad way, is the way I saw it. It was the first time I'd looked at him and thought that there's something desperately wrong here, er, he just looked sad, fed up with life and fed up with his condition and fed up with everything. His eyes were stained, the whites of his eyes were stained and he was fixated on me, which was very unusual for Jacob, he wouldn't normally stare at anything or anyone for any length of time, and he was, which is when I first went in and said, 'Are you all right, Mucker?' meaning, 'Are you OK?' and obviously there's no response, but three or four times after that I've said 'Are you OK Jacob, are you OK?' and I was holding his shoulders and trying to get him to respond, I guess, but there was no response, apart from him just looking at me.

QS Had he been as unresponsive as that before you went away to Iraq?

A No, he was, er . . . he looked desperately sad that day.

QS Would you describe him as 'happy and lively'?

A No, not for the last four years, um, there was . . .

QS On that Saturday?

A No, definitely not.

QS So what did you do?

A Um, I spent some time with Jacob and then, er, I think I went in to Mary to see how she was getting on and she said, 'Well, he's quiet, you may as well go, there's no point in you hanging around.'

QS Did you say anything to Jacob?

A No, just 'Goodbye', as I normally would, and give him a hug, but no, I didn't say anything.

QS So you went out and saw Mary and she said?

A Er, 'He's quiet in his room, there's no need for you to be here any longer.' I'd been there for a while and she said that, er, I could go.

QS What was in your mind when you left and you had seen him in that state, what were you thinking?

A Um, I really don't know at that stage. There was nothing particularly that I was thinking about, apart from [pause] how advanced he'd got with the disease. That was . . .

QS So what did you do?

A I left the bungalow and went down to the TMG Club again, on the way ringing Gary Vine to see if he was going to join me.

QS We heard his statement read. And what were you doing at the TMG Club?

A Er, we were just chatting about normal things that we chatted about to start with, er, we were drinking. Er, at one stage I did start talking about Jacob and my frustration with, er, his equipment, his incontinence pads were – were not sufficient for his allocation, we didn't have enough and it was always a battle to try and ration them so that we wouldn't run out before the end of the quarterly allocation or monthly allocation.

QS So these are practical concerns. What about other comments, did you make any?

A Yes, I think, um, er, it had been playing on my mind, because I did say to him, I think, 'Jacob's not there any more.' I think I said something along the lines of 'Jacob's gone, he's not there any more, and he doesn't recognize me.' I'm not sure.

QS Is that something you would normally have discussed with Gary Vine?

A No, never, he was very unaware of Jacob's condition and my family life as it was.

QS So why did you choose that day to discuss Jacob's condition with Gary Vine?

A I don't know.

QS Did you discuss Jacob's condition with anybody else, any of your other friends?

A No, sir.

QS Do you easily discuss your domestic situation with other people?

A No, sir.

QS Did you talk to Mary at all that Saturday, after you had left the house and you were down at the club, did you talk to Mary at all?

A Yes, er, shortly after I'd been talking to Gary Vine, um, I was still thinking about it and although I was trying to be as cheerful as I could it was still playing on my mind, so I decided to ring Mary about what I had seen when I spent the time with him in the bedroom that day and I went outside the TMG and I rang her.

QS And told her what?

A I said to her, er, 'We need to talk.' She said, 'I agree.' I said, 'You know what I'm talking about?' She said she did and then she said, 'You're talking about Jacob, aren't you?' and I said 'Yes', er, and I said, 'I think he's had enough, Mary, I think he's come to the end of the road. I don't believe he recognizes me any more. I think his quality of life is . . . is not worth anything to him. I don't think he's there, I think Jacob's dead, I think he's gone.'

QS What did she say?

A She totally agreed and said, um, that she wasn't sure how much . . . how much longer she could cope with the situation and, um, and watch him deteriorate any further. At that stage we had to cut the conversation short because we were both getting emotional, Mary more so, because apparently Jacob was – she said to me that Jacob was with her when she was talking to me and she was getting very upset, because, obviously he was with her, and so, er, we ended the conversation there with, I think she said, 'Have you spoken to anyone about this?' and I've said 'No,' I said, 'No, I haven't,' and she said, 'Don't mention this to anyone.'

QS Jacob, of course, was deaf?

A Correct.

QS So he couldn't hear what you were saying to Mary?

A No, she was, er, implying . . .

QS Or what she was saying to you?

A It was upsetting her not him, it was . . .

QS And you had been at the club. How much had you had to drink at this stage?

A It's hard to remember exactly how much I drank but it's, er, yes, I drank a fair bit, quite a bit, but I did not feel at any stage . . . probably [pause] three pints maybe.

QS Were you in any way drunk?

A Not at all.

QS Are you used to heavy drinking or not?

A Um, when I drink I drink a fair bit, I would say, but not . . . I don't drink every day, I don't have a problem with drink.

QS I don't expect you to remember times, but roughly what time was the first telephone call to Mary?

A Between four and half-five, I would say . . . I really don't know.

QS Did you call her again?

A Yes, I called her approximately an hour later . . .

QS Why?

A I wanted to talk in more detail about what I'd been talking about with her and about Jacob's condition.

QS Before you got to the telephone call, what had you been thinking about in between the two telephone calls?

A Just about Jacob, but I don't think I was actually thinking about anything apart from I needed to speak to Mary again to see exactly what she felt.

QS Were you discussing it at all any further with Gary Vine?

A No.

QS . . . What was the conversation between you and Mary on the second call?

A I said to Mary that I'd been, er, I was very concerned about Jacob's state at the time and that I felt that I could do something for him, meaning I could end it for him.

QS Were you specific?

A Yes, I said that, um, I was going to take the holiday in Gran Canaria for a week, consider my options, but the likelihood is that I would think about it, come back, take Jacob away with me and then make a call to the police and then a call to Mary to say that it was all over for him, at which point she said, um, 'Why wait?' and I replied, 'Well, I need some time to think about this.' I think, or something along those lines, and that, er, that was – we did talk in length, but I can't remember the exact context of that conversation, but it was about Jacob and Jacob's condition.

QS Regardless of what she says she meant by, 'Why wait?' what did you understand her to mean?

A If I was going to – if I was considering doing this why would I not do it straight away, why – why wait and go on holiday and think about those things and have that on my mind, you know, I don't know, but that's what I assumed she meant. [Pause] And at that stage as well in that conversation she said to me, um, 'Could you do this for the family?' and that's when I replied, 'I'm not doing this for you. I'm not doing this for me, I'm going to do it for Jacob.'

QS Did you say you said to her you were not doing it for her?

A Correct.

QS Not doing it for you, you were doing it for Jacob. And what was her response to that?

A I can't remember.

QS Can I just deal with the possible beneficiaries of the action you proposed. You said you were doing it for Jacob?

A Yes, sir.

QS Why?

A Because, um, I didn't want him to suffer any more than he already had and I wanted him to die with dignity in the place where he was most loved and most comfortable, um, and that's what happened.

QS And did you think he was at death's door or anything like that at that particular time?

A No, sir, but I felt he was days away from being very, very uncomfortable and in a great deal of pain.

QS So that would stop him going on that path. What about Mary? You have said it wasn't for her benefit?

A No, sir.

QS . . . and you said you weren't doing it for yourself?

A No.

QS I think you told Mary that you were going to go to the police immediately after you had done it? . . . Or call the police? What benefit can you see yourself gaining from this action?

A None.

QS What did you expect to happen when you rang the police?

A Um, that I'd be stood here one day, having to ex –

QS And what did you think would happen to you?

A I thought I would go to prison, sir.

QS Help us, would you. The action has been described as 'selfish'. Can you see any benefit to yourself from the action, which I am coming on to in a moment, that you took that night?

A No, sir.

QS At the end of the second telephone call to Mary, did you talk to anybody else about this idea which you had discussed with Mary?

A No.

Andy went on to say that after his second call to Mary he returned inside the club but told nobody of his conversations with his wife.

QS Did you display any concerns? These things were going round in your head, did you discuss these any more with Gary? Did you . .

A No, I tried to act as normally as possible under the circumstances, and, er, I tried to put it to the back of my mind.

QS Did you continue drinking?

A Yes.

QS What were you thinking about?

A Um, I was just thinking about what I'd discussed with Mary and whether it was possible and whether it was right for him.

Andy then testified that he accompanied Gary and his girlfriend to two other public houses – he said he did not have a drink at one and only had, as far as he could recall, one at the other.

QS How would you describe your state?

A I wasn't drunk . . .

QS Were you able to walk all right?

A Yes, absolutely.

QS And how was your speech?

A Fine . . . I left Gary and Anita. I don't remember saying goodbye to them, I just got up and left.

QS Once you got outside into the air what happened there?

A That's when I made a third call to Mary.

QS What did you say?

A I stood outside the pub, rang Mary and said, 'Get George up, take him to your mum's, it's tonight.'

QS Did you elaborate on that at all?

A Only to say, 'Make sure you take George in to say goodbye and you say goodbye to Jacob.' And I said, 'I will call you when I get nearby so you can leave with George.'

QS Had you made the decision by then?

A Yes, I think so.

QS When you said to Mary, 'It's tonight', was there any doubt in your mind as to what that meant?

A Absolutely none, because she said, 'Oh my god', um, and I think she must have been passing George's bedroom as she said that, because she said, 'Oh, George is still awake', meaning it wasn't a problem to wake him up, and no, absolutely none, she knew exactly what I meant.

QS Could you have done what you did without Mary's approval?

A Never, no.

QS Had you ever asked Mary to take George out of the house in the middle of the night before?

A No, sir.

QS Did she question it at all or say, 'Why should I take George?'

A No, sir, she didn't.

Mary was sitting at the back of the court listening to her ex-husband giving evidence. Although at no time during the trial did she appear to have eye contact with him, at this stage of his evidence, for some reason, Andy appeared to be distracted by her.

QS Please don't be distracted by Mary in court. If she distracts you then I shall make an application.

Andy described how, after telling Mary to prepare to leave the house with George, he quickly walked home.

QS You told Mary that you were proposing to terminate Jacob's life, without specifically using those words, of course, but, referring to that, had you made up your mind as to when it was going to be, when it had to be done?

A By then I think I had, yes.

QS You said you had a call from Mary. Where were you when that was received?

A Just on the corner of Henty Road . . . I said she could leave and, er, I think she re-confirmed exactly where I was because she didn't want to leave Jacob unattended for too long . . .

QS Did she say whether or not she intended to leave him alone, albeit for a short period of time?

A Yes.

QS Was that at your request?

A Yes.

QS Why did you want neither of them in the house when you went in?

A Er, two reasons. One was to, um, protect George, and the other was to protect Mary so that she wouldn't be incriminated, that she wasn't going to be there.

QS Did you get to the house?

A Yes.

QS Was it locked?

A No, the door was open.

QS Do you mean physically open or unlocked?

A It was unlocked and closed.

At this stage of Andy's evidence, of course, I knew what he was about to describe. I can't remember what my feelings were at that precise moment. Andy and I had not discussed the details of Jacob's death to any great extent prior to the trial, as I knew that doing so would only serve to upset us both. This was the first time I was to hear the tragic details.

QS Tell me, please, what happened when you went into the house?

A I, um, went straight through the front door and turned left into Jacob's bedroom. Um, he was asleep in bed.

QS Were there lights on in his room?

A I can't remember, I think a dimmed light was maybe slightly on but I can't remember, um, [pause] I went, er, straight over to his bed.

QS Was he awake or asleep?

A He was asleep.

QS Fast asleep or . . .

A Fast asleep.

QS What did you do?

A I took a pillow from the side of him, er, it wasn't under his head, er, because that would have disturbed him, I took a pillow from beside him, um, [pause] and then, um, I knelt across him, put the pillow over his face and then I lay down with him on top of him.

QS Was there any movement, any struggling?

A None.

QS When Jacob was breathing, we have heard that he had very impedimented airways, did he breathe noisily when asleep?

A Very noisily.

QS Tell us, how long was it before he didn't make any noises?

A He, um, he didn't make any noises from when I put the pillow straight over his face.

QS So, immediately?

A Immediately.

QS How long did you lie there with him?

A I don't know, I don't know. It wasn't long.

QS How did you feel?

A [Pause] I felt, um, [pause) I felt a sense of relief that it was over, um, and then I was just shocked, I couldn't tell you what I was thinking, um, very, very, very um, upset.

JR 'Very, very, very'?

A Upset.

QS How did your being upset demonstrate itself?

A I was crying, er, I would say I broke down.

As Andy explained to the court what he had done, many of the jury members, the journalists, the people in the public gallery and myself, were again in tears. I was glad Anne was not in court at that time.

While giving evidence, which he did in a quiet, controlled manner, Andy was obviously upset. He paused on several occasions and took a sip of water to compose himself when it seemed he may break down.

(While I have been typing this I have been listening to background music, as I often do. Just as I started writing the passage where Andy entered his house to end Jacob's life, the most beautiful, but what I think is one of the saddest pieces of music started to play – the Intermezzo from *Cavalleria Rusticana*. I have been moved to tears just listening to it in the past, but strangely, not this time. As I have continued to record the details as Andy related them in court, I looked up at Jacob's photo above my desk and I feel sure he was saying, 'Don't be sad, Grandad. Daddy loved me and I am HAPPY.' I am not religious, but I cannot really explain this – perhaps there is no need to.)

QS You told Mary that you were going to call the police?

A Yes.

QS Did you?

A No, she, um, she said she didn't want me to because she wanted to spend some time with him.

QS So how did you speak to Mary?

A I rang Mary, um, twenty minutes, half an hour afterwards, because I wanted to spend some time with him myself, um, and that was spent just stroking his head, talking to him, trying to explain why I felt, um, that it was the best thing for him, and then after about twenty minutes, half an hour, I called Mary to say that it was all over and that I was going to call the police and she said, 'Don't call the police yet, wait until I get home.'

QS Did you desist from calling the police until she got home?

A Yes, sir.

QS You have told us that when she came back you were still in the room?

A That's correct.

QS With Jacob, is that right?

A Yes.

QS What happened when Mary came into the room?

A She came into the room and said, 'Oh, my god'. I moved back from Jacob, um, so she could spend some time with him, which she did, then she, er, after I don't know how long, she turned round to me and hugged me.

QS She hugged you?

A Yes, sir. Then we spent time together with him in the room and then we moved into the kitchen before, er . . . where I believe she poured some wine.

QS Did you drink wine? You say she poured wine, poured wine for herself or for you or both of you?

A For both of us.

QS And did you both drink wine?

A We did, we did, and it was at that stage I toasted Jacob and said, 'He's at peace, he's with Henry now.'

QS Did Mary exhibit anger with you at all?

A No.

QS Did you call the police?

A We went back in with Jacob and spent some more time with him and then I called the police.

QS We have heard the record of your calling the police, and I need not take you to that. When the police arrived there were attempts, we have heard, to resuscitate Jacob. I don't want to take you all through it, but is it right that both of you tried to stop the police from resuscitating Jacob?

A Yes, sir.

QS One matter I think I didn't ask you about: years beforehand, when Jacob was first diagnosed as having Hunter Syndrome, you used to go up to Manchester to the consultants? On how many visits did you go?

A I remember four, possibly five, but I was there for a few.

QS And there was evidence of a discussion that you and Mary had with a lady and, I think, her daughter called Abigail . . . Was there such a conversation?

A We had a conversation, yes.

QS Do you remember what you said, if anything, during the course of that conversation, about Jacob?

A No, sir, I don't.

QS Do you remember saying anything about how one could deal with the situation in which the mother of Abigail and yourselves found yourselves?

A No, I mean, um, the little girl in question was very, very ill and was days away from dying, and I don't remember any conversation like that and I just don't think that I would say that, under the circumstances, because Jacob, obviously, was reasonably well at that time.

QS Stay there please.

And that was the conclusion of Andy's evidence-in-chief. My feelings at that stage were that Andy had come across as a good witness and I know that his defence team thought the same. Andy had been clear with his evidence and, although not outwardly showing his emotions a great deal, his feelings were, I thought, conveyed to the jury

Chapter 9
Cross-Examination

I think that most of us, including the jury, who had sat in court over a period of two days listening to Andy's evidence, must have been completely drained by this stage. I know I was. It was dramatic, traumatic and heartbreaking and I was pleased that Anne, who was waiting in the witness room with the others who were later to give evidence, did not hear all the graphic details.

I was a little surprised that the judge did not decide to call a short break to the hearing between Andy finishing his evidence-in-chief and his cross-examination by the prosecution.

The majority of lawyers, during their career, represent both prosecution and defence and some specialize in one or the other. The prosecution are instructed by the Crown Prosecution Service and the defence by the solicitor representing the defendant. When barristers are questioning either defendants or witnesses while they are in the witness box they do, of course, have to adhere to strict rules, and if they do not then the judge will direct them accordingly. It is the job of the barrister to extract the truth from the witness and defendant and at times it can appear that the questioning is harsh and a personal matter between them. In many ways, lawyers are actors, they have a script and a story and they have to present their case in the best and most professional way they know how. They all, of course, have a vast knowledge of the particular part of the law in which they specialize, and one cannot deny that they do, at times, like to score points when questioning defendants and witnesses. Yes, sometimes the questioning does appear to be put in such a way as to trip up the defendant or witness, but it is done with the sole intention of hearing the truth, in order that the jury can reach a fair verdict. Many of these points were displayed by both Mr Sayers and Mr Katz.

Mr Philip Katz QC then began his cross-examination of Andy.

QK Mr Wragg, yesterday morning you heard a number of witnesses tell this jury, from Naomi House, and Chestnut House, you heard those people describing Jacob's condition during his respite care in July just before you killed him?

A Yes, sir.

QK Do you disagree with what they had to say about Jacob?

A Yes, sir.

QK You do?

A Yes.

QK You disagree with it?

A Yes.

QK They gave an account of a child who had this terrible condition but who was quite capable of enjoying himself and his life and was doing so. You disagree with all that?

A Completely sir, yes.

QK Completely. So those people caring for him at that time, you just didn't see the same picture?

A No, sir.

QK Let's deal with you, Mr Wragg. You were asked a moment ago by your counsel about whether it was a selfish thing that you did – all right? And you said 'No', because you were going to call the police and you thought you would be standing in court one day. If you were asked to describe yourself generally would you say you were a selfish person?

A Yes, at times I'd say I was.

QK Do what you want to do?

A At times.

QK Irrespective of the wishes of your wife?

A Yes, sir . . .

Mr Katz continued to pursue the question of Andy's selfishness, to which he agreed. He then turned to the plans Andy had after he was to return from Iraq a second time.

QK Was Mary, or the children, to play a part in this future?

A Yes, sir.

QK Was it? They were, were they? They were to play a part in this future?

A Yes, sir.

QK You came back and you had planned, you say from before you even went, that you would have some time on holiday on your own?

A That's correct.

QK When you came back you had a few days with Mary and George at Center Parcs?

A Correct.

There were more questions about Andy booking a holiday in Gran Canaria, to which he gave the same answers as he did to Mr Sayers and stating that '. . . this was discussed with Mary and she . . . she agreed and was fine with it, which is why she went ahead and booked the holiday in Center Parcs.'

QK Yes, but what you did, Mr Wragg, was once you had got back [from Iraq] you spent time with your friends drinking?

A Yes, sir.

QK Because you wanted to?

A Yes, sir.

QK You didn't go straight home and spend time with your wife and children?

A No, sir.

QK Because you didn't want to?

A No, sir.

Mr Katz then returned to questioning Andy about going to Center Parcs and booking a holiday for himself in Gran Canaria.

A . . . It is something we'd discussed before I left and it's something that I did.

QK 'Something we'd discussed'?

A Uh-uh.

QK Or did you just tell Mary that you had booked this holiday and you were going?

A No we discussed it before I left for Iraq and then I booked it whilst I was on leave, which, yes, she wasn't happy about.

QK But you ignored her unhappiness and you made the plan anyway and that's what you were going to do?

A I did, and I also offered her to have time on her own while I spent it with the boys once I returned from Gran Canaria.

QK And when you got back, during those days, you were drinking regularly to excess, weren't you?

A Er, no sir, I was not working, and therefore I would be drinking more than if I was working, yes, but no, I wasn't drinking to excess.

QK It wasn't a very happy period between you and Mary during those days, was it?

A Er, no, sir.

QK No. You told the jury you spent at least one night away from home. That's right, isn't it?

A Yes, sir.

QK And so you come back. You are having a social life. Is that right?

A Yes, sir.

QK Sleeping all right, were you?

A [Pause] Reasonably, yes.

QK Yes. Eating all right, were you?

A I'd lost two and a half stone in Iraq, but, yes, I was eating better.

QK Eating better once you got home?

A Yes.

QK Yes. Socializing with your friends?

A Yes.

QK Not spending days alone in bed, not wanting to get out of bed?

A No, sir.

QK Thinking about the future, a holiday, a job?

A Yes.

QK Yes. You were still interested in sexual matters, weren't you?

A Yes. Sir.

QK Yes. Mr Wragg, can you tell the jury, please, in what way your life, when you came back from Iraq, was particularly different from your life before you went?

A Jacob's condition had changed remarkably. That's the big difference in my life when I got back from Iraq, is the change I saw in Jacob.

QK But your life, the life you were leading, what you were doing was no different was it?

A No, sir.

QK And Jacob, you felt, didn't recognize you when you got back from Iraq?

A Yes, sir.

QK You hadn't been around a lot, had you?

A No, sir.

QK So when you get to the position, Mr Wragg, when you are thinking about your future before 24th July, after you get back from Iraq, what was your plan for your future and your family's future?

A Much the same as any other family's. We planned, er, a possible extension on the roof to extend the bungalow. Um, I wanted desperately to clear my debts and support the family as I should have done and sometimes didn't, and make Jacob and George's – you know, Jacob as comfortable as possible and give George the things he wanted and needed.

QK So let me understand this; at the stage you get back from Iraq it is still in your mind that Jacob has a future?

A Before I get back from Iraq, yes.

QK When you got back, after you got back?

A No.

QK Well, when do you say, Mr Wragg, because you tell us that you had this time with him on the Saturday afternoon while you were at home while Mary was having her nails done, what sort of time did you spend with him between getting back from Iraq and 24th July?

A Not a lot, sir.

QK Five minutes?

A No, longer.

QK How much time did you actually spend just with Jacob during those days?

A We were living in the same house, sir, we would have spent time together.

QK Well, he was, as we have been reminded, in respite care from 12th to 22nd.

A That's correct.

QK You got back to the country on the 9th. Is that right? What day do you say you got back home?

A The following day after my flight in from . . .

QK Well, was it the following day or was it a day beyond that?

A It was the following day, sir.

QK So that takes us to the 10th or the 11th, at any rate?

A Yes sir.

Mr Katz continued to question Andy about the length of time he had seen Jacob after returning from Iraq, which Andy agreed was not a great deal.

QK What are you saying then, on that afternoon (11th July) you spent with the family, that's when you decided this boy had no future?

A No, sir.

QK And you were going to kill him?

A No, sir.

QK Right. So on that afternoon, when you spent more time with him, what was in your mind about Jacob and his future?

A I didn't know what his future was. I just [pause] thought I should think about his future for him.

QK You should think about his future. Did you discuss with Mary about what she thought about his future?

A Later on in the day, yes, four times.

QK Sorry?

A Later on in the day we had four conversations where this was brought up, and four times she agreed that she felt the same way and this was the best thing for Jacob.

QK I am sorry, which day are we talking about now?

A Sorry, the 24th.

QK No, I'm talking about this afternoon?

A OK, sorry.

QK You get back on the 9th and you say you got home on the 10th or the 11th?

A Sir.

QK Jacob has gone to respite care on the 12th, out of the picture, from your point of view?

A He was at respite care, he wasn't out of the picture, sir.

QK All right, he wasn't out of the picture, but you were not with him?

A No, sir.

QK . . . You go off to Center Parcs . . . With Mary and George?

A Yes, sir.

QK Right. I want to know, please, this period of time, however long it was, you have said an afternoon with the family, I want to know, please, are you saying you discussed then with Mary what Jacob's future was?

A No. Sir, we didn't.

QK No. Are you saying that afternoon before you went to Center Parcs, before Jacob went to respite care you decided to kill him, that he had no future?

A No, sir.

QK No?

A It was mentioned at Center Parcs. One night when we were out we did talk about Jacob's future and we did talk about the – the difficulties in bringing him up and trying to look after him. Mary expressed a lot of concern about his future.

QK Well, she was the one with the difficulties, wasn't she, Mr Wragg?

A That's right, sir.

QK Practical difficulties?

A Yes, sir.

QK Your son, but she had the practical weight of all this, didn't she?

A Yes, sir.

QK Now what was the purpose of Naomi House, Chestnut House, when it gets to the end and the child is really about to die, there is a phase when they give palliative care so that the child may die in dignity?

A Yes, sir.

QK And you are saying, are you, that your choice gave you more dignity, are you?

A I am, sir.

QK My Lady, that is an appropriate moment. There is a matter I have to raise with your Ladyship.

JR Can we manage without the jury, then?

QK Yes.

JR Mr Wragg, first of all, you go back to the dock. You cannot discuss your case with anyone, you are giving evidence, so you return for the moment. Ladies and gentlemen, this is something I can deal with without you. You go and come back to us at two o'clock. Don't forget the warnings I always give you.

The jury filed out. The prosecuting counsel then made a lengthy application to the judge to be allowed to introduce into the case evidence that had been disallowed by her at an original application, very early in the trial. This evidence basically centred on whether or not Andy had a girlfriend with whom he spent the night in London on the day he arrived home from Iraq. If the prosecution could prove he did, then they hoped to question his credibility generally and besmirch his character. Mr Sayers objected strongly.

QS My Lady. I have to say that I am surprised at my learned friend waiting until now to make this application when Mary Wragg is no longer giving evidence . . . As I understood it the agreement was . . . all references to his dealings with other women, and indeed, her possible dealings with other men, have been left out of this trial as being irrelevant to the issue which the jury have to deal with. I am no longer in a position to deal with Mary Wragg, but my learned friend always knew that he [Andy] would say upon his return from Iraq he spent time, which is true, drinking with his friends in London. That was to be anticipated . . .
. . . My Lady, I thought this case was about the killing of Jacob Wragg. What my learned friend is asking, I would suggest, is an attempt to bring in issues which might besmirch his character in front of the jury and are not directly relevant. I repeat the subject of my application to your Ladyship at the outset: whether he has got a girlfriend or not bears no relation to what his plans are for the future of the family; it is naive to suppose that because someone has a passing affair during the course of a very unstable marriage, that that means they do not propose at that time to continue remaining married and giving a home to the children. We must not forget that Mrs Wragg had already started divorce proceedings, and this was a temporary return to family life to see if it worked, and the mere fact that my learned friend is anxious to get in this piece of evidence, that he spent the night of his return

with another woman, can only be in order to try and blacken his name. It really has no bearing, we would submit, on his state of mind, which occurred later on after his return from London, when he made the dreadful decision to end his son's life, and I would repeat that submission to your Ladyship. It is probative of absolutely nothing but creates a lot of prejudice. Had it been in evidence before, and my learned friend knew this was going to happen, never going to be anything else, if the defendant gave evidence that was always going to be the way we dealt with it, and I am precluded from dealing with it with the wife.

Mrs Justice Rafferty then gave her ruling.

JR Mr Katz. I follow entirely the Crown's position, but I am not going to let you explore this for these reasons: I agree that Mr Wragg has set himself up as being a man with a benign eye to a united family future, one has to be a realist. The jury may take a different view of extramarital conduct from the view it takes of drinking with friends and holidays alone. [The second reason was concerned with the evidence which was to be given by one of the psychiatrists.]

Following the luncheon adjournment, the Jury were recalled and Andy went back to the witness box. Mr Katz continued to cross-examine and he took Andy through his army record, which was not disputed, particularly asking him about a letter from the Chaplain stating that Jacob would benefit from stable domestic arrangements. Andy agreed that at times he did not get that. Andy agreed that we had all been involved with fundraising for Chestnut Tree House and he did know of the palliative care provided by the Hospice.

QK Did you have it in your mind that if things got to a point where you thought something had to be done you would intervene and put a pillow over his face?

A No, sir.

QK Did that never cross your mind?

A Once or twice, when he was very young, very young, but no, not in the months leading up to his death, no.

QK Well, let's go back to once or twice when he was very, very young. You do agree, do you, there was an occasion when you were in Manchester and Jacob was there being treated . . . There was another mother . . . the daughter was called Abigail . . . who was a very, very, very poorly child . . . Genuinely possibly correctly described as being at death's door.

A That's correct.

QK And her mother, tell me if this is right, because this was Mary's account to the jury, by the stage at which this was all happening, she, the mother was rather wishing the doctors would leave her child alone to die. That was the gist of it, wasn't it?

A . . . Yes, sir.

QK Did you say something along the lines . . . 'I won't let Jacob suffer. I'd rather put a pillow over his face?'

A No, sir, that would have been totally inappropriate because Jacob wasn't at that stage very ill, her daughter was.

QK . . . Well then help us, please, as to what you meant a few moments ago when you said when he was much younger some thoughts along those lines crossed your mind?

A I refer to the time when he was diagnosed, the week after his diagnosis, and talking to the family and Mary, er, about how I would not like to see Jacob get to a situation where I thought his quality of life was not there any more, and that I would consider helping him by terminating his life.

QK Right. So it wasn't on the occasion when Abigail was, you say, involved, but you agree, do you, that you have said something along the lines of you would help Jacob if it got to that point when you didn't want to see him suffer any more?

A Yes, sir, we both said that.

QK You are not saying Mary said she would do it, are you?

A I'm saying that we would make the decision together, yes, that's exactly what I'm saying.

QK Or is this you after the event, Mr Wragg, trying to implicate Mary in what was your decision?

A That's for the jury to decide . . . But I'm telling you, yes, she was completely aware of what was happening that night and it would never have happened if she had expressed at any time that she did not want that to happen.

QK Are you suggesting that over the years that intervened between Jacob's diagnosis there was an ongoing agreement between the two of you that you would end Jacob's life if it got to the point? Is that what you are saying?

A Yes, yes, that we would seriously consider it if we felt that his quality of life was not there any more.

QK You are saying this was something that was agreed between you from day one, was it?

A It was talked about, and what I am saying is that we both agreed. It wasn't mentioned much, it was mentioned in the early days and I don't remember it being mentioned after his fourth birthday at all, but it may have done – mentioned it, and, as far as I was aware, we were both of the same opinion.

QK This just isn't true, is it, Mr Wragg? This just isn't true?

A It is, sir . . . I would not take that decision alone . . . Mary was Jacob's mother and as much as, er, my thoughts for her now are she was a good mother to Jacob and George and still is, um, and I'm just telling the truth.

QK . . . I think you told the jury this morning, was that Jacob had days to live?

A No, I said – I think I said that I, um, felt he was days away from being in serious trouble and serious pain, not necessarily that he was going to die in the next few days.

Mr Katz then spent some time cross-examining Andy about his evidence, the point of which was to imply that he had planned Jacob's death for some time (which would indicate murder rather than manslaughter), and that it was not a decision made on his return from Iraq. Also, that Jacob was killed in an act of selfish drunkenness without Mary's knowledge. Andy totally denied this, as he had in his evidence-in-chief.

I am not going to record here the entire transcript, because a large part of it was about whether Mary was aware of Andy's decision to end Jacob's life or not. In fairness, Mary was not on trial, and is not here. I have merely tried to record the facts fairly and in a balanced, objective manner. Mr Katz also seemed to labour the point of exactly where the pillow used to end Jacob's life was taken from, his purpose being to question why Andy could remember some things but not others.

QK You had planned how you were going to do this, hadn't you, Mr Wragg? You knew exactly how you were going to do it?

A No sir, I didn't know.

QK You thought about how you would do it, you made your decision, you got Mary out of the way and, in accordance with your plans and your careful plans, I suggest, you went home and did what you thought was necessary in your mind. That is what you did, isn't it?

A It's what we . . . it's what we both wanted and that's what happened . . . And I also believe that it's what Jacob wanted . . . Because I saw in his eyes that he'd had enough and that his suffering was awful, and I couldn't tell if he was in pain any more.

QK Mr Wragg, you did this for yourself, didn't you? It was a selfish killing and you did it in drink?

A No, sir I did not.

QK You realized the consequences of what would happen, obviously the police would be involved, but you made the decision, you made it rationally and you did what you planned to do?

A No sir, if I was selfish I'd have walked away.

Andy was then re-examined by Mr Sayers. He confirmed that he ended his son's life in order to stop his suffering. He said that Mary made the majority of decisions involving the family, especially involving the children – that she 'wore the trousers' in the family – she was the primary carer.

QS You were asked questions about your plan for the family's future when you returned to live at 68 Henty Close. Yes? Were you aware that Mary had already started divorce proceedings?

A No, sir.

QS Were you given any indication as to whether or not she had asked for these proceedings to cease?

A No, sir

QS To abandon them?

A No, sir.

QS . . . Do you claim to be the ideal father?

A No, sir.

QS Do you claim to be the ideal husband?

A No, sir.

QS It was put to you that Mary did not say at any stage, 'What are you waiting for?' Do you remember that?

A Yes, sir.

QS But you said that is what you understood her to be saying? . . . I just want to ask you in respect to that bit of conversation.

Mr Sayers then referred the jury to part of a police interview with Mary in which she admitted saying to Andy 'What are you waiting for?' She said to the police 'I don't mean "what are you waiting for", I mean what is Jacob's life going to be like in the future.'

QS . . . did she say something like that on the phone?

A That's exactly what she said and it was clear to me what she meant.

QS And finally this, about the questions you have been asked about Mary. You answered Mr Katz saying that you didn't want Mary in the house so that she wouldn't be implicated. Mr Wragg, are you aware that whether or not Mary was implicated, what sort of impact that would have on your own position, your own guilt or innocence?

A No, sir

Andy's testimony was concluded.

A great deal of time was taken up in the trial with testimony from the psychiatrists, Dr Gillian Mezey for the prosecution, and Dr Peter Wright and Dr Matthews for the defence. The first two appeared in person and spent several hours in the witness box – Dr Matthews did not attend due to ill health, but gave evidence by written statement. What they said was most interesting. Much of it was very technical and revolved around the medical definition and interpretation of 'diminished responsibility'. In addition to the medical professionals' opinions, the lawyers' legal opinions and interpretations of the law relating to the subject were argued at length, sometimes in the absence of the jury for legal reasons.

The doctors' evidence highlighted the problems juries have when being addressed by what are called 'professional witnesses'. All three psychiatrists had consulted with Andy at great length and gone over the same ground with him – his childhood, family background, upbringing and marriage, also, and most particularly, his time in Bosnia and Iraq, and the events leading up to Jacob's death. They described at some length what they understood to be post-traumatic stress and quoted statistics and examples.

Ultimately, Dr Mezey's conclusion was the opposite of that reached by the other psychiatrists. All three agreed that Andy was probably not suffering from post-traumatic stress disorder or mental illness, but they were unable to agree as to whether Andy was suffering from what is known as acute reaction to stress and adjustment disorder, which could affect his mental state and rational thinking. The two defence psychiatrists concluded that in their opinion he was, and the disorder probably played a large part in his actions on returning from Iraq. The prosecution psychiatrist, however, did not agree, and her view was that adjustment disorder was a very minor and temporary condition and could occur after losing a job, getting divorced or moving house.

That opinion was strongly challenged by Andy's QC Mr Sayers, who questioned that an analogy of such events in one's life compared to what Andy had experienced was inappropriate.

The outcome of Andy's trial rested on the state of his mind when he ended Jacob's life. His defence was that he was not suffering from a mental illness but that his mind was affected by events he had witnessed and experienced and thus a 'diminished responsibility' plea was appropriate. The prosecution disagreed and would not accept such a plea.

Mrs Justice Rafferty seemed to make certain that the members of the jury could follow the complicated medical evidence, but whether they fully understood it all I doubt – at times I found it difficult. During my days in the police I have been in court on many occasions when expert witnesses have contradicted each other and there are recent cases where there have been miscarriages of justice due to the opinions given by such witnesses. It is hardly surprising that juries can be swayed by the mere fact that they are called 'expert' witnesses, and in such cases it follows that the verdicts are often decided on opinions rather than facts. Andy's case certainly was one of those. With professional witnesses with years of experience unable to agree, it was left to each individual jury member to arrive at their own conclusion.

Then it was the turn of family members to give their evidence. Apart from Steve, none of them had testified in court before, and they had been waiting for several days in the witness room in anticipation. They were good witnesses, all describing how they had known Jacob all his life, some seeing him more regularly than others, but all loving him dearly and describing with sadness his deterioration over the years. Steve and Chris gave very succinct evidence and were not fazed when cross-examined by Mr Katz. I felt sorry for my daughter, Tina, who had seen more of Jacob than the others, and had in fact seen him just prior to his death. She described him as 'like a zombie' the last time she saw him. She said he was very vacant and didn't seem to recognize her. Mr Katz implied that the expression 'like a zombie' was disrespectful and derogatory, but Tina said it was the only word she could relate to the way he was.

It was decided that Anne's evidence would not be challenged and her statement was read to the jury. Several of Andy's friends who knew Jacob also gave evidence – some in person and some by written statement – about Andy's relationship with Jacob and of watching Jacob's gradual regression.

Mr Katz summed up the case for the prosecution. He concentrated his argument on his belief that Andy had not told the truth, that he was manipulative and had killed Jacob in a selfish, drunken act. He asked the Jury to find him guilty of murder.

Mr Sayers, summing up for the defence, relied mainly on two points: firstly that Andy had always told the truth throughout and secondly that, in his opinion, the overwhelming evidence from two psychiatrists was that Andy was suffering from diminished responsibility at the time he killed Jacob, and he believed that it was an act of mercy and love from a father who saw his son suffering terribly. He invited the jury to find him not guilty of murder.

The judge then summed up the case for the jury. She went meticulously through the evidence for both prosecution and defence. She asked the members of the jury to consider the case purely on the evidence and not to be swayed by any emotional feelings. Her Honour said that, quite simply, they had to decide if Andy was suffering from diminished responsibility or not. If 'yes' then a verdict of manslaughter could be given, if 'no' then the verdict must be one of murder.

The jury retired to consider its verdict at 11 a.m. on Wednesday 16 March. By 4 p.m. they had not reached a verdict and were sent home for the night. They re-sat the following morning and at 12.23 p.m., Mrs Justice Rafferty, in answer to a written question from them, explained the criteria needed for an abnormality of mind sufficient for a defence of manslaughter.

Two hours later the court was recalled and the judge explained to the jury that she would accept a verdict upon which at least ten of them agreed.

During this time we were waiting in the witness room, with Anne who had come to hear the verdict. It is hard to explain all our emotions. Andy had brought a bag with him with a few possessions, expecting to go to prison. He had photographs of Jacob and George and I'd given him a small radio. We all made quiet conversation.

The court building was packed with press and media awaiting the verdict. Many wished Andy 'good luck'. The street outside was also packed, with radio and television reporters, two vans with satellite dishes and numerous photographers, some from abroad.

With Andy and the rest of the family's agreement, I had prepared two statements to give to the press, one in the event of a guilty verdict and one for a verdict of not guilty.

At 4.25 pm, the word went round the court, 'The jury are coming back.' There was a mad rush back into court by the media and the public, and we all made our way to our seats. Andy stepped back into the dock. As the members of the jury made their way back to the jury box, I tried desperately to decipher from their faces anything that would give an indication as to their findings – of course there was none. I held Anne's hand tightly on one side of me, Tina's on the other. Chris, Sara and Steve were sitting behind.

Then came the bombshell – the foreman of the jury stood and told Mrs Justice Rafferty that they had not reached a decision and there was no chance of them doing so.

To me, that only meant one thing, a re-trial, but then Her Honour addressed Mr Sayers and Mr Katz and said something that possibly indicated her feelings and certainly gave us all some hope for a fairly quick conclusion to our nightmare. She said, 'It seems to me entirely reasonable for the Crown to have the opportunity to stand back and draw breath.'

To us, and indeed to Andy's legal team, that statement indicated that Mrs Justice Rafferty was suggesting she thought a charge of 'manslaughter on the grounds of diminished responsibility', to which Andy would have pleaded guilty from the outset, should be seriously considered by the Crown Prosecution Service.

We knew that such a decision would take a little time, but with that in mind, Andy returned to live with Chris and Sara, Steve went home to America, Tina, Anne and I went back to Worthing, all to carry on our lives, but all still left in limbo.

A week later we received the disappointing news that the CPS would not accept a plea of manslaughter, and had decided to proceed to a second trial on a charge of murder. Who exactly made that decision, I do not know. I was informed by a police source that, along with the Crown Prosecution Service and their lawyers, the other people consulted would have been the police officers involved in the case, and Mary.

On that latter point, it should be remembered that once the police had decided not to charge Mary with any offence, without her evidence they had virtually no case against Andy except his own admission. Had Mary decided not to give evidence against Andy, or even refused, the Crown could have made her a 'hostile witness', which is something they are usually very loath to do.

In view of the nature of the crime and all its possible legal implications for the future, my feelings are that the final decision to proceed to a second trial on a charge of murder was made by someone with great authority in the legal profession in this country. The interest of the public would no doubt be a consideration in view of the emotive nature of the case. Also, the possibility of the case being quoted as a 'stated case' sometime in the future may have been considered. In English Law, as part of their submission, lawyers sometimes quote previously reported cases, usually involving a judicial decision. In other words, 'stated cases' set a precedent and are used as a guideline. Because of the many unusual features of Andy's case and the legal arguments that arose, it could well be referred to as a 'stated case' in future trials.

Perhaps I am wrong, but I do have very good reason to believe that, even up to the first day of the second trial, the Crown were still being advised to seriously consider not proceeding on the charge of murder and allowing Andy to plead guilty to the charge of manslaughter.

For whatever reason, and I cannot believe it was because they felt they had a strong case after the first trial, they again arraigned Andy on the murder charge.

Chapter 10
The Second Trial

Between the two trials we all tried to lead as normal a life as possible but found it difficult.

For eight months we continued to have the same restrictions as we had awaiting the first: we had to be careful not to have any dialogue with prosecution witnesses, and we were still not permitted to see George. Our lives were put 'on hold' again. The time just seemed to drag and the prospect of enduring the traumas of another trial was always at the forefront of our minds.

We did have some happier moments though. Anne has been a nurse since qualifying in 1964. We met while she was training at the West London Hospital, Hammersmith and I was in the Metropolitan Police – why, I wonder, do so many policemen marry nurses? Apart from taking time off to have our children she has worked more or less continuously. Up until 2005 Anne nursed for approximately thirty-three years at the same private hospital in Worthing, Goring Hall. She retired on 14 January 2005 and the hospital staff gave her an official retirement party with a number of presents, the main one being a lovely set of garden furniture. Unlike me, Anne is an excellent gardener and is fanatical about it. She spent many hours in the garden during our sad times and found it most therapeutic.

In addition to the official retirement party another surprise party had been planned for Anne by her close friends to take place in January 2005. It was to be attended by relatives, friends, doctors and surgeons from Goring Hall with whom she had worked for years – all had so kindly contributed. I had liaised with the organizers over the months, obviously without Anne's knowledge.

The problem was that we were not exactly sure when Andy's trial was going to take place and a venue for the party had to be booked well in advance. I discussed it with Paul and Brenda Murray, the main organizers, and once we knew that the trial was set for February we decided to book the party for April 2005. We obviously talked about the possibility of Andy being found guilty and serving a prison sentence but we decided that whatever the outcome the party for Anne should go ahead – life had to go on and it would lift her spirits if only for a few hours. Consequently a hotel was booked in Worthing for about one hundred and fifty people.

The conclusion of the trial on 24 March with the jury unable to reach a verdict, again presented a dilemma for the party organizers: to go ahead knowing that we were all still in limbo, having to await another trial, or to put everything on hold? We decided that we should continue as planned.

The result was that Anne enjoyed a fabulous surprise party and met up with friends whom she had not seen for many years, including one of the bridesmaids at our wedding. Many of our family attended and although Andy would have liked to have been there he did not come as he would have breached his bail conditions. Anne was presented with a 'This is Your Life' book showing photographs of her nursing career since 1964. The amount of work and planning that went into that party was phenomenal and Anne said that the evening gave her a great deal of happiness during such a dark period of her life.

The possibility of holding the second trial at the Central Criminal Court, Old Bailey was discussed but we were pleased when that did not happen – we would not have been happy to travel to London each day.

During the period between the trials, Mr Sayer's junior barrister, Mr Bailey, was replaced by Ms Kate Lumsden, and both she and Louise Colwell from the solicitors, did a great deal of work preparing for the second trial, which began at Lewes on 28 November 2005, again before Mrs Justice Rafferty.

The jury comprised eight women and four men; all seemed, on average, middle-aged, some presumably with children.

Mr Sayers represented Andy and Mr Katz appeared for the Crown.

The second trial was much the same as the first with one big difference. The judge directed that the case should be about Jacob's death and nothing else. She did not want any part of the trial developing into a family court as had happened at the earlier trial, so much of the evidence that had been given then relating to Andy's and Mary's relationship was omitted.

Her Ladyship even instructed Mr Katz, prior to Mary giving her evidence, to warn her to testify only on subjects about which she was asked. As a result, in the witness box Mary was more composed than in the first trial, and she did not openly display any mementos of Jacob. Mary still refuted some of Andy's evidence and in particular that she knew of his intention to end Jacob's life.

The arguments were the same as in the first trial – the prosecution suggesting that Jacob's death was a selfish act committed for his own benefit and the defence saying he did it as an act of love to end his suffering. Once again a lot of time was taken up by the psychiatrists' evidence – one suggesting that Andy was not suffering from diminished responsibility and two saying that he was.

In the second trial, as in the first, the tension and emotion in court were electric as Andy repeated his emergency call to the police; when he described the termination of Henry's life, and when he told of ending Jacob's life. Many of the jury were in tears, and although I had heard it before, so was I.

Andy gave evidence in a controlled manner, as he had in the first trial, but more succinctly and less hesitantly. He seemed to be more confident in his cross-examination by Mr Katz.

It is not necessary to repeat in full the evidence Andy gave at his second trial as much of it was very similar to the first; however, it is of interest to know of some of the answers he gave when being cross-examined by Mr Katz. These are taken from the report recorded in Court by Louise Colwell and are used here by kind permission of Edward Hayes, Solicitors.

A great deal of Mr Katz's cross-examination seemed to concentrate on two things; first, that Andy was lying when he alleged that Mary knew he was going to end Jacob's life and agreed to it happening, and secondly, that Andy was also not telling the truth about the number of telephone and text contacts he had with Mary on the night Jacob died, or about the content of those messages. Mary, it appeared, disagreed with what Andy said about these matters.

Mr Katz asked, 'Have you changed your account deliberately so these matters were going to not come out?'

'With respect sir, I am the one that called the police, I told them I have taken my son's life,' Andy replied. 'What I say about Mary is what happened. I am the one standing in the dock, sorry if you get the impression I am changing my story, sorry but the truth is the truth and I am not changing that.'

When it was suggested that Andy was mistaken about the time he had spent with Jacob on the afternoon of Saturday 24 July he replied, 'If you are going to ask me about how long, time is irrelevant to me, it's the content of that meeting that was important to me.'

Andy described seeing Jacob's condition on that afternoon as a 'life-changing experience'.

Mr Katz questioned: 'Did that life-changing experience ever happen?'

Andy confirmed vehemently that it did.

Mr Katz asked why Andy had not in his initial interviews with the psychiatrists mentioned to any of them anything about Mary giving him positive encouragement to kill Jacob.

'No, for the good reason that I was still protecting Mary. Then she made her second statement in which she was trying to destroy me.'

Asked about his interview with Dr Mezcy, expert witness for the prosecution, Andy concurred that he did say that he did not feel guilt about what he had done, but he denied that he said he would 'do the same again' as 'there would never be another situation like Jacob'.

As in the first trial, Andy agreed that the marriage was volatile throughout, that he left home at times, and that the stability Jacob got was mainly down to Mary.

Andy told how he thought Jacob had not much quality of life during the last year of his life, and he disagreed with the hospice staff on that subject, pointing out that he saw far more of Jacob than they did. He described Jacob's sad condition when he returned from Iraq, saying,

'He had changed a lot. He didn't appear to have recognized me, he was sleeping longer, he had a lot more mucus, his face was deformed. His skin on his face was stretched.,

Andy described the events on the day Jacob died and of going out for a drink with Gary Vine and other friends.

He again told of his frustration with the social services that he had voiced to Gary.

Mr Katz asked him, 'You said, "Poor old Jacob, looking into his eyes today I don't know if he knows what I am saying. They limit him to three incontinence pads a day and he is through them by morning." Is the reality that your principal complaint, as spoken to Gary Vine, was that you were not getting enough help?'

'Yes in view of the fact we did not have enough incontinence pads,' Andy replied.

In the absence of the jury a lengthy legal discussion took place involving a further statement of Mary's, together with videos and photographs that had been served on the defence by the prosecution just a few days before the start of the second trial.

On behalf of Andy, Mr Sayers objected strongly to the new evidence being used. His defence team had spent many hours looking at it. The videos had been edited by Mary and only selective footage of Jacob had been used, most of it showing him when he was much younger and little of him in recent years. Mr Sayers pointed out that he would want to see all, unedited, videos from which the edited version had been made and that would take a considerable amount of time.

Mrs Justice Rafferty agreed and did not allow the new evidence to be put to the jury.

Mr Sayers also drew to the judge's attention the fact that in his closing speech to the jury at the first trial he had said: '. . . whether or not Mary was complicit doesn't affect it at all, whether she was or not doesn't really matter.' He went on, 'I made it clear that we were not concerned with what went on in her mind but only what was going on in the defendant's mind. The decision was made by me to avoid the circus last time when allegations were flying out of the witness box, which were deeply unattractive.' He had, he said, chosen to avoid all these issues in the second trial so as not to be drawn into an emotional battle between Andy and Mary.

The witnesses were mostly the same as in the first trial, although several, where there was no dispute as to what they were saying, did not attend and their statements were read to the jury.

Tina, who was several weeks' pregnant, was one of those due to testify again, but sadly the night before she was to stand in the witness box she suffered a miscarriage.

Her Ladyship expressed her condolences and, with the agreement of Mr Katz, Mr Sayers read Tina's statement to the jury.

Anne – who had not given evidence in person at the first trial – did do so at the second.

Nervous as she was while waiting to be called to the witness box, once she was in it, she was splendid. She spoke so obviously from the heart that she could only win sympathy. She said how much she had loved her grandson Jacob, how she had seen him choke on a number of occasions and how it broke her heart to see his physical and mental states deteriorate. Her evidence was not challenged.

Both Mr Sayers and Mr Katz addressed the Jury in their closing speeches as they had done in the first trial, and Mrs Justice Rafferty summed up the evidence very succinctly, as before. She also told the jury not to be influenced by the fact that Andy was not the sort of person who showed his emotions greatly in court. She said that he did not show them openly, but that did not mean that he didn't have any – some people are like that.

She explained to them the alternative verdicts to the charges of murder or manslaughter.

The jury retired to consider their verdict on the afternoon of Monday 11 December; once again, they had not reached a decision by 4.30 p.m. and were sent home for the night.

By the next morning we were in a state of acute anxiety. At the first trial, Anne had found the experience of waiting for the verdict and its announcement so traumatic that she could not face going through it a second time; she just wanted to be alone, she could not bear the thought of seeing her son sent to prison for life for murder. Andy was quite happy that she should not be there, so we agreed that she should stay at home and await our phone call.

Andy arrived at court bringing with him a bag of personal belongings in anticipation of going to prison; he seemed quite resigned as to his fate and outwardly showed no signs of what he must have been going through inside.

The press and media were again there in force and wishing him luck.

The jury resumed their deliberations. After approximately an hour – bringing the time spent considering the case to four and a half hours – they returned to court.

Andy was told to stand as the clerk addressed the jury, 'Foreman of the jury, please stand. Have you reached a verdict upon which you are all agreed?'

'Yes.'

At that moment I noticed Andy looking up and staring at the ceiling.

'On the charge of murder, do you find the Defendant, Andrew Wragg, guilty or not guilty?'

'Not guilty.'

'On the charge of manslaughter on the grounds of diminished responsibility, do you find the Defendant, Andrew Wragg, guilty or not guilty?'

'Guilty.'

'And is that the verdict of you all?'

'Yes.'

I could feel my heart pumping, Tina and Chris squeezed my hands, Steve patted me on the shoulder and tears rolled down my cheeks.

I glanced at Andy and I noticed him look towards the jury and give a slight nod.

Mrs Justice Rafferty then told the court that she was going to adjourn as she wanted to give some consideration to the sentence she was going to pass.

We all again waited outside the courtroom but there was a noticeable feeling of relief amongst us knowing that Andy was not guilty of murdering Jacob.

Steve immediately phoned Anne to tell her of the verdict – a great relief to her, as it was to us. But of course we still all had another agonizing wait to know the sentence.

While we were waiting, I talked to Andy and he said something which I shall always remember: 'Dad, did you notice that when I was waiting for the verdict I was staring up at the ceiling? Well, I was, in my mind, talking to Jacob. I was saying to him that if I had done wrong then it was him who was going to punish me, it was him who was going to send me to prison, not the jury, not the judge but Jacob. I know he will see I'm OK whatever happens.'

I put my arm around his shoulder and said, 'Don't worry Andy, you loved him, you'll be OK, you're strong enough to handle this.'

He was still expecting a prison sentence and prepared for it – anything less than five years, he thought, was an acceptable term to serve, given what he had done.

After two hours of interminable waiting we went back into court, which was once again packed, to hear the sentence. Mary was also there to witness what was going to happen to her ex-husband.

The judge instructed that nobody was to leave the court until she had finished passing sentence. She would, she said, give the press a copy of her fairly lengthy sentencing statement.

"Mr Wragg, my sentencing remarks are quite lengthy. Will you remain seated please, until I invite you to stand.

Andrew Wragg, I deal with you for the taking of your son Jacob's life at a moment when your responsibility for what you did was diminished as a consequence of an acute stress disorder and adjustment disorder. You are no threat to the public. I treat you as of good character.

Killings range from the actions of the sadist to those of a man who, as a mercy, kills a loved one in response to a plea for release from a terminal illness. Although Jacob was unable to make such a plea to you, I accept that your genuinely held belief was that what you did would bring to an early end a life afflicted and drawing inexorably to a close without intervention. Jacob was vulnerable by virtue of his disability and age and you held, as to him, a position of trust.

Mitigating factors are that what you did was an act of mercy, that you reacted to stress you found insupportable, and that you have, from the moment you telephoned the police, admitted what you did. I give you maximum and generous credit for that honesty, as I remind myself of the evidence called by the Crown that Jacob's airways were so obstructed that without your admission a death certificate would have been signed.

Your then wife, late that night, removed your younger son from his bed and drove, via a late opening shop, to a lay-by where she stopped the car. Only after you had telephoned her with the news that Jacob was dead did she drive on to her mother's flat and, without any prior arrangement, leave George with her.

One would have to be quite remarkably naive to accept that this dedicated and experienced mother behaved in that way solely so as to enjoy an evening of prolonged intimacy with you. I have no doubt that she was complicit. Had I concluded otherwise, I should have formed a harsher view of you. I accept that you would not have taken Jacob's life had you for a moment thought that she disagreed with what you were to do.

In my judgement, what you have done and said since you killed Jacob imported to begin with a desire to shield and protect her, as did your instruction to her to quit the house before you arrived, so that as far as you could you guarded against incriminating her. All who listened to the evidence must have wondered at the remorseless strain Mary bore lovingly and bravely during the ten years she dedicated to Jacob, as you concede you did not so consistently do.

I shall sentence you loyal to what you have always said: that you did not do it for her, or yourself, but for him.

You served your country in a successful army career which you gave up out of love for your family. In my view, it was when you quit that life, which demanded structure, and which recognized valour, that your path to this court began. With hindsight, you, and Jacob, and Mary, and George would have been better served by the experienced support and discipline of your Regiment had you stayed. You would almost certainly by now have been commissioned into a service career of distinction.

Stand up, please.

No matter your motive, the end of Jacob's life was not in your gift. I am well aware that the sentence this court passes cannot be measured against the loss of him, nor should it be. Mr Sayers, Queen's Counsel, told the jury that you took your son's life as he stood at the gates of his last dreadful journey. No words could better have caught the mixed tragedies with which I have to grapple.

For all the reasons I have set out, your case seems to me exceptional. That being so, I consider there is nothing to be gained by taking from you your liberty.

Sending out, as I sentence you, the resounding message that this was not a mercy killing but a deed done by a man suffering from diminished responsibility, the sentence of this court is of two years' imprisonment suspended for two years. Sit down."

Mrs Justice Rafferty did not make any order or recommendation regarding Andy receiving psychiatric treatment or counselling.

There is no doubt that in years to come Andy's case, and the sentence in particular, will be quoted and argued by lawyers as a 'stated case' in trials involving altruistic filicide.

Although the law is different in America, Andy's trial and sentence are mentioned on the internet with particular reference to a case in the United States, in which a father went to prison for ending the life of his terminally ill disabled child.

I did not see Mary's reaction when the sentence was announced.

Mrs Justice Rafferty then advised Andy to leave the dock but to wait with his legal team and family until the court had cleared. He came straight to us, his family, and put his arms around us; then he shook hands and thanked Mr Sayers, Louise Colwell and others of his lawyers.

We left the courtroom together and waited in the corridor for several minutes. I noticed that most of the journalists were on their mobile phones, presumably speaking to their newsrooms. Some were attempting to obtain interviews or statements from Andy and the rest of us, but we refused to say anything to them and explained that I would be making a statement outside the courthouse shortly.

Many people congratulated Andy; he politely thanked them but it was very noticeable that there was no celebrating amongst us. We felt that this was not a time to celebrate – of course we could not have been more pleased with the verdict, but overshadowing all this was poor Jacob whom we had loved so much and whose loss we had not had time to grieve.

Steve phoned Anne immediately we knew the sentence and, fighting to keep my voice from wobbling, I then spoke to her. I have asked her what her feelings were at that moment and she says she just can't describe them adequately, she had so many mixed feelings – love for Andy, love for Jacob, love for all her family and a tremendous relief that our nightmare was finally over.

When we had all composed ourselves I went to the steps of Lewes Court together with Steve, Chris and his wife Sara, and Tina and her husband Max. Andy stayed on with his lawyers in the courthouse. He said that he would never publicly speak about the case and to this day he has not.

In front of me was a sea of photographers, journalists and television cameras from various media companies, including the BBC, ITV, and Sky. I have no idea how many microphones were pushed in my face.

I read a short statement that had been agreed with Andy and the family, saying that we were pleased with the result of the trial, thanking the jury and Andy's legal team, particularly Mr Sayers, and asking that from then on our privacy be respected in order that we could now grieve the loss of Jacob and get on with our lives.

Regrettably not all the press adhered to that request.

We all adjourned to the White Hart Hotel opposite the court, where Andy joined us a short time later. After, I think, just one drink, we all left Lewes for the last time and returned to my house where Anne was waiting.

Once the verdict had been announced on the national news broadcasts, the phone did not stop ringing for the rest of the day as relatives and friends rang to express their love for us and their happiness at the news. Our neighbours, too, were wonderful, calling at the house with champagne, wine and cards. Anne and I will always be grateful to them for their kindness and support..

In the evening, we all went to a local restaurant for a meal, after which Anne and I , utterly exhausted, returned home. Steve, Andy, Chris and Sara, Tina and Max stayed on.

They all came back to the house at about eleven o'clock. Anne was up but I had gone to bed, and I think I was half asleep when I became aware that Andy was in the room. He sat on the bed, put his arms around me, hugged me and said, 'Dad, I love you, I will never be able to thank you enough for what you and Mum have done for me.' He then left the bedroom and closed the door.

I cried quietly. I had never known Andy to express his feelings like that before and I will remember the moment for the rest of my life.

Chapter 11
After the Trial

Once the second trial was over we all settled down to something like a normal life. It could not be completely normal, though, given the antics of the press – which I shall come to later – and our trips to the High Court in London to apply for access to our other grandson, George.

Because of what happened to Jacob,and the interminable delays by the family court, social services, CAFCASS (the Children and Family Court Advisory and Support Service) and others, Anne and I were prevented from seeing George for more than two years after his brother's death. Also, Mary had various objections which she obviously believed were in George's interest. I disagreed with some of her reasoning and views but respected her right to them.

Because of his frustration in the delays, on several occasions Andy reached the point of not wanting to continue his fight to see his son and it was apparent that the stress was beginning to tell – his morale was at a very low point at that time and he resigned himself to the possibility of not seeing George for several years, but holding on to the belief that after his eighteenth birthday George would seek his father out. However his lawyers, Anne and I persuaded him there was light at the end of the tunnel and he decided to continue with his application for access.

It was evident that Andy's application to see his son was going to take much longer than ours, therefore Anne and I thought it right that we should see George, not only because we loved him, but also because we believed strongly that the family link and bonding with the family should not be lost. Because of what he had been through with the loss of Jacob, we realized that things should not be rushed, but we thought that over two years was questionably too long. George was getting older and had lost contact with our extended family.

When we were finally granted an access order and went to see him he appeared fine and was overjoyed to see us all again, particularly his cousin Ella, and our little dog whom he had not forgotten having had so much fun with in the past.

On professional advice we did not discuss Jacob with George, but we were well prepared to answer his questions if asked. He was still receiving bereavement counselling, but Anne and I were not given any information as to how that was proceeding as evidently such advice would be a breach of client confidentiality. We were never the less very much aware of the necessity to treat any situation with George delicately. We obviously had a number of photographs of Jacob around the house, but George never mentioned him except once, when he saw a photo of him on my mobile phone and commented, 'That's a nice picture of Jacob.'

It was nearly three years after Jacob's death before Andy was allowed to see George, but when he finally did the father-and-son bonding was evident, apparently unaffected by their time apart. Andy now sees George on a regular basis and they both seem very happy.

When Jacob was born and before he was diagnosed with MPS, Mary's dad opened some kind of bank account which was to pay for his private education when he was old enough. Although Jacob was unable to benefit from Ron's generosity, George has been able to and he is now a pupil at an excellent school and is doing well.

On 30 June 2006 Andy and I drove up to Hereford. The following day was the anniversary of Henry's birth and death.

The two days we were in Hereford were the longest time I had spent alone with Andy, since Jacob's death, and we talked a great deal about what had happened in our lives during the past few years.

We spent the first day in Hereford visiting the various places that had been part of Andy and his family's life when they lived there. We went to the SAS headquarters where he had been based, and we also visited the house they had lived in – a house that had sad memories, for it was there that the family were living when Jacob was diagnosed with MPS and when Henry's life was terminated.

There were happy memories, too, though, because Jacob was HAPPY. Looking into the garden of that house it was easy to remember Jacob running around, kicking his ball, teasing the dogs, playing with his toys and splashing in his paddling pool during hot summer days. It seemed like only yesterday . . .

Andy and I went to the park where Jacob used to play and the children's playground where he loved to go – I have a picture of him on the swings there, looking so happy.

We also walked to the lake where Jacob had run into the water to retrieve the bread Andy had thrown to the ducks.

In the evening we met up with a friend of Andy's from the security company he had worked for in Iraq. It did him good to catch up with news of people he had worked with but, even then, he was to learn that one of his former comrades had been killed after he had left Iraq.

The following morning we had breakfast at Hereford Swimming Pool where Andy had taken Jacob on numerous occasions when on leave. For me too it had memories – when Andy had been in Bosnia, Anne and I had spent some holiday time in Hereford, and I had taken Jacob to the pool. I remembered so well Jacob laughing as we went down the water slide together and catching him as he jumped into the pool – he was fearless. Afterwards, I recalled, he thoroughly enjoyed a plate of chips and a strawberry milk shake in the cafeteria.

After breakfast Andy and I bought some flowers and went to Hereford Cemetery where Andy had no problem finding Henry's tiny grave in the children's section. It was a little overgrown and unmarked, which I found rather sad. Mary and Andy have said that they would like Henry to be reburied with Jacob in Worthing. Whether that can come about one day I do not know, but if not, I would like to think that eventually a headstone can be placed on Henry's grave in Hereford.

It was pouring with rain as Andy placed the flowers for his son, who had died in the womb in order that he should not suffer in life and so that Jacob could receive as much love and caring from his parents as was possible.

I left Andy alone with Henry for a few moments and as I did so I looked around at all the small graves, and thought of all the heartache each one of those plots must represent.

My mind went back many years to when Andy was just two years old and Steve was five, when their baby sister, Joanne, died very suddenly at the age of eight months from pneumonia.

I recalled Anne and me walking behind her tiny white coffin in a total daze and I had some idea of what Andy and Mary must have been going through when they buried Henry, different though the circumstances were.

Andy joined me in the car and we began our long journey home.

He was quiet for a few minutes, deep in his own thoughts, but then we began to talk.

We talked a great deal about Jacob and about George's future.

From the chat that we had one thing stuck out and, on reflection, cemented even more my belief in my son – although not for one moment have I ever had any doubts about his motives for ending Jacob's life.

As a police officer I saw and heard many examples of accused persons and witnesses who, for various reasons, made untrue statements to the police and told lies in the witness box. Invariably when that happens discrepancies occur which will be highlighted in a trial, especially if there are two trials. It is very difficult for a person, if not telling the truth, to stick to the same story when asked to repeat it.

Here are some of the things that Andy said on the way back from Hereford, which I wrote down when I arrived home:

'Two years prior to Jacob's death we used to lie in bed and listen to him coughing and choking. Sometimes we would discuss leaving him to die but we never did. We just hoped we would find him dead in the morning. He was suffering so much.'

'I helped him to stop choking many times. I saved his life but nobody gave me any credit for that.'

'Not many Hunter's boys have such a peaceful death.'

'I wanted him to die with dignity in the place where he was most loved and most comfortable.'

'I saw it in his eyes, his suffering was terrible. He couldn't talk but he looked at me and his eyes were telling me he had had enough.'

'Jacob will punish me if I have done wrong.'

'I still sleep with my arm over my ear as I used to do to block out the sound of Jacob's poor breathing. I suppose now it is just habit.'

The reader may recognize most of these quotes – from my notes of our car journey – as being much the same as those from the transcript and accounts of the trials.

What Andy told the jury at both trials did not vary and there were no relevant discrepancies that were challenged by the Crown. Had there been, Prosecution Counsel would certainly have picked up on it and probably suggested that Andy was lying.

His account of what happened and why has never varied, whether when he was speaking to the police, to the lawyers, the court or us, and it confirms my solid belief that Andy ended Jacob's life because he wanted to put a stop to his suffering – for no other reason.

As regards the future, the saying 'time heals' is possibly true, but one can never, or perhaps should never, forget the past. It is pointless living with regrets because one cannot change what has gone before but it is important to learn from our mistakes.

Andy and Mary, like most of us, no doubt regret some of the things that have happened to them during their lives, particularly regarding Jacob, but I believe for George's sake it is important for them to move on. They appear to be doing that gradually, both have new partners and seem content.

Andy has moved away from Worthing but now sees George on a regular basis and both are very happy when together.

Andy still takes life as it comes and whatever it throws at him he bounces back. He had a very good management job for a year but was made redundant overnight when the company went into administration. He immediately applied for positions with other companies, was accepted by one and had actually started work having been told by them that they were not concerned about his conviction, which he obviously divulged and explained in detail. Twenty-four hours later, however, the company reversed their decision, which really upset him. He understands that an employer may have reasons not to employ him but he feels that once having made a decision they should not renege on their decision without giving him a chance to prove himself. He has since found employment with another company, where he is happy and progressing.

Nobody knows what tomorrow will bring. I know Andy has plans for the future but does not worry about it – he takes after me that way. I have always believed you can do nothing about yesterday, but you can ruin today worrying about tomorrow. Worrying never solves anything, logical concern can.

When we lost our daughter, Joanne, Anne and I did not have counselling but we benefited a great deal from talking to friends and relatives. Andy has never had counselling, either, and, because of his introverted nature, appears to find it difficult to let his true feelings come to the fore. Since Jacob's death there have been occasions when he has appeared depressed and I do worry about him – sometimes I think that maybe a professional adviser would benefit him. George has had some bereavement counselling and I am sure that it will be of benefit to him, but I do not know whether Mary has, and it would not be right for me to comment.

Anne and I are at peace now and, considering the devastating events and experiences we have been through since the police knocked on our door on that dreadful day in July 2004, I think we have survived pretty well – a few more grey hairs perhaps !

Thanks to our beloved little Jacob, though, we have learnt how much the true love of family and friends means. And while life goes on much the same, we think about him and talk about him daily. We laugh and we cry, but are ashamed to do neither.

Chapter 12
The Press

In 1839, in his play *Richelieu*, Edward Bulwer-Lytton wrote 'The pen is mightier than the sword', and in a country where we more or less have freedom of the press no truer words have probably ever been written.

We all know of numerous examples where the press have ruined or greatly improved people's lives, sometimes by just a few headlines, other times by continued coverage and publicity. Since 2004 my family and I have had many dealings with the media and press in one form or another and I feel our experiences qualify me to give an objective opinion on them.

Let me say from the start that generally I felt the press and media dealt with the reporting of the death of Jacob and the subsequent trials respectfully and fairly. The 'red top' papers printed the usual headlines one expects from them, but I am fully aware that they all have a job to do, they have stories to report, deadlines to meet and newspapers to sell.

Only after the second trial did the style of reporting seem to change because whilst it was going on the journalists had plenty to report that was coming from the courtroom, whereas at the conclusion, columnists and regular writers were free to voice their opinions on everyone and everything sometimes with little regard for what had been said in court. I will come to this later.

We had some dealings with the press, particularly the local papers, over the years before Jacob's death. Mary submitted several articles to magazines about Jacob and Hunter Syndrome and how it would dictate their lives. The local press also reported details of Jacob's illness, his prognosis and how Andy and Mary were coping. One story that was reported involved the theft of a toy car that Jacob loved to sit in and push himself along with his feet. Within a few days of the story appearing in the *Worthing Herald* newspaper, and with their help, the generosity of an anonymous person and the Early Learning Centre, an identical car was given to Jacob. He was delighted. We never knew who that person was but we continue to be grateful for the thoughtful and kind gesture. The local papers also reported a number of the fund-raising events, including 'Anne's bridge jump' and the charity football match that Chris organized; the opening of Chestnut Tree House was also covered by local papers, with photos of Jacob and George, every article helping to bring Hunter Syndrome to the public's attention.

Following Jacob's death the national press coverage became part of our lives.

It was clear early on that the press realized that not only did they have a story about Jacob's death that would be headline news for several days but, as time went on, and particularly during the trial, there was the obvious conflict between Mary and Andy with her denying any part in their son's death, giving the reporters great copy.

Within hours of the police informing us of our grandson's death reporters from national newspapers were knocking at our door. How they got our address so quickly I don't know but with a name like 'Wragg' I suppose it wasn't difficult. I just politely told them I did not wish to comment and they left. Within a few hours Chris arrived and, working in the media himself, he was ideal to handle the situation for which we were very grateful.

Our first real experience of what we were to face came on the morning of Andy's initial appearance at Chichester Court. I was with Chris, Sara and Tina and as we approached the court we could see an army of press photographers and an array of flash bulbs exploded. How they knew who we were I don't know, they just seem to be able to sniff you out. Inside, the court was packed with reporters, not only sitting in their press box, but standing at the back.

They quickly realized that Anne had stayed at home, and she later told us that two people had knocked on the door who were obviously reporters as they put their cards through the letter box. We had told her not to answer the door, and she sat on the stairs distraught and in tears until eventually she phoned her mother and asked her to come over and give her some comfort, which she did.

On leaving court we were accompanied to our cars by the police and returned to Worthing where three reporters were already waiting. Chris informed them that we would make no comment other than that we supported Andy and requested that they respect our privacy and leave us to grieve the loss of Jacob.

Between the time of Andy's arrest and his trial hardly a week went by when the press or media did not contact us by calling at the house or by phone, although how they obtained our phone number I don't know because it is ex-directory – that's their job I suppose.

All of them obviously knew that they could not publish or broadcast anything that involved the case as it was *sub judice*, but their main object at that stage was to prepare for stories after the trial had concluded. The newspapers wanted every aspect of Andy's life, what it was like to live with a Hunter's boy, what it was like for Anne and me to have a son who had ended the life of our grandson – anything that would sell newspapers. We received many letters from national newspapers and magazines, some of them offering us huge sums of money if we agreed to give them exclusive stories at the end of the trial.

Most of the national television channels approached us, *Panorama*, *ITV News* and the *Trevor McDonald Programme* all wanting to explore the possibility of making programmes about Andy and the pressures of bringing up a child with MPS. Some offered payment – of course if Andy was convicted of any offence he could not receive remuneration for anything relating to it. We declined all offers.

We heard of press reporters going to great lengths to obtain stories from various people. One of Andy's ex-girlfriends whom he was with for a short time during his separation from Mary was offered money for her story and when she refused one of her work colleagues was approached. Two of Andy's old school friends were contacted and even Vicki Hammel, who conducted Jacob's Remembrance Service and burial, was phoned in America.

A local newspaper reporter, Paul Holden, who was at school with Steve and who knew Andy, Mary and Jacob, having met them at the odd social gathering, because of his closeness to the family did not become involved in the reporting of any of the events. Instead, he kindly gave me advice which was invaluable in my dealings with the press throughout.

Another former school friend of Steve's, Eddie Mitchell, a freelance photographer, became a good friend to Anne and me. On most days during the trials he was outside the court with all the other press and media; a very imposing figure six feet six inches in height, he seemed to have a certain amount of control over the press pack. On occasions it seemed as though he was orchestrating their behaviour and was at the front preventing them from harassing us too much as we entered and left the court . We were grateful for that.

Paul and Eddie's integrity was also shown towards the end of the trial when photographs of Andy with Jacob were released to the press. From the outset the press and television displayed photographs of Jacob, some on his own, many with Mary but none that I ever saw with Andy. Most were photographs taken sometime prior to his death, but I do not know their source. Anne and I received requests from just about every national newspaper for pictures of Jacob and Andy and were offered large sums of money for them but we declined.

A decision was made by Andy's legal team that up until the end of the first trial no photographs of him, either with or without Jacob, should be given to the press. They did not want any suggestion that the jury might be influenced by anything they saw or read in the press. Only when the jury had been out deliberating their verdict for a day did Mr Sayers authorize us to give photographs to the press.

That evening Eddie Mitchell came to our house, looked at our many family photographs showing Andy and Jacob and copied them. He then discussed with Paul Holden what they had and it was obvious that the collection of photos would be worth a great deal of money to them. However, true to their word, they arranged for them to be released to the Press Association at no charge and the Association released them to the national papers. The result was that a number of lovely pictures of Andy and Jacob were printed. At no stage did Eddie or Paul receive any money for photographs or articles involving Jacob's death and I thank them both for their integrity and professionalism. It is a pity that some other people in the press and media do not follow their example occasionally.

Anne and I, Andy and most of our family were photographed pretty well every day, entering court, leaving court, even at lunch times.

During his trial Andy stayed with friends in Brighton and travelled to Lewes quite early. We met him each day at an old hotel, The White Hart, immediately opposite the court, for breakfast. He would cross the road a little before us to attend a daily conference with his lawyers and each time he would face the flash bulbs of the photographers. We faced the same when we went across. Each day in addition to the press there was the media with their transmission vans parked in the High Street and in the White Hart car park. Both BBC and ITV carried daily live reports on the progress of the case in their lunchtime news bulletins.

Every day as we waited for the court to sit the many press reporters gathered and were always polite. I came to recognize many of them – a few of them I had spoken to before, when they had called at our home. One or two introduced themselves to us and asked if we wanted to make any comment but did not pressure us when we declined.

On the first day of the trial several came up and quietly wished Andy, Anne and myself good luck. Over the days as more and more evidence evolved it was noticeable that the number of reporters who wished us luck increased and one, from a national newspaper, said to me, 'Everyone in the press box is behind your son.'

We were careful not to have any lengthy conversations with them or be seen to be especially friendly but we were polite and acknowledged them and they seemed to appreciate that.

Anne, especially, was quite upset during the early days of the trial as all the headlines and media reports appeared to paint a bleak picture of our son and alleged torrid reasons for his ending Jacob's life. Of course the press were only reporting what had been said in court and for anyone not familiar with the workings of the English legal system it is important to understand that the first part of a trial is taken up with hearing the case for the prosecution. It obviously sounds very biased against the accused and I had to keep reminding Anne that the picture would completely reverse once Andy's defence was heard, as indeed it did, with the headlines and reports giving much more favourable accounts.

On the final day of the first trial the press and media interest was at fever pitch. They were all gathered anticipating a result and the court was packed. When, after deliberating for eleven hours, the jury told the judge that they could not reach a verdict on either the charge of murder or manslaughter and were discharged, and nothing definite was announced as to whether there would be another trial, it was to the press something of an anti-climax as the case had to still be treated as *sub judice* and the same rules about reporting still applied. As usual we were asked for comments but made none.

As I wrote earlier, when the first trial ended on 17 March 2005 without a verdict, it did appear, from comments made to both Prosecution and

Defence Counsel by the judge suggesting that a certain course of action might be taken in agreement with the Crown Prosecution Service, that a plea of 'guilty to manslaughter on the grounds of diminished responsibility' might be acceptable. For a week, both we and the press were in limbo. Then, on 24 March, the devastating news that the CPS would not accept a plea of manslaughter and were going to proceed to a second trial on the charge of murder.

Once this decision had been announced officially the press coverage began again. We had visits at the house and phone calls asking for our reaction to the news of a second trial – as usual we made no comment. These became less frequent but as the trial date – 28 November 2005 –approached two or three journalists from national papers called and asked me to consider giving them exclusive rights to our story at the conclusion of the trial in return for large sums of money. Even my daughter, Tina, was door-stepped by a reporter with the same offer. I made it quite clear that nobody in my family wanted to sell our story to any newspaper.

Although the conduct of the second trial was somewhat different from the first, the media coverage was pretty much the same. We recognized most of the journalists, and they treated us with politeness and respect. While the jury were deliberating, several journalists wished Andy and me good luck. For the verdict the press box was packed and many reporters either sat in the public gallery or stood at the back of the court.

Prior to taking the verdict and sentencing Andy, Her Honour Judge Rafferty stated that she did not want anyone leaving the courtroom until she authorized them to do so. This applied to all the family and those connected with the case including the press. The reporters were obviously desperate to hear the verdict and get their stories out but the judge did not want a 'mad rush' occurring. She told the journalists that she had prepared a sentencing statement, which she would read out and a copy of which would be given to each one of them.

That statement – which I have quoted in an earlier chapter – gave a succinct account of Judge Rafferty's assessment of the trial and her reasons for imposing a suspended sentence and was printed the following day in all the national newspapers.

As I mentioned earlier, it had been agreed with Andy, Steve, Chris and I that, whatever the outcome, I would read out a prepared statement to the press and media. I wrote two while awaiting the jury's verdict, one for a 'guilty' verdict and the other for a 'not guilty' and Andy had OK'd it.

Following the verdict and sentence there was chaos as reporters rushed out of the courtroom, most getting on their mobile phones giving their stories to their respective newsrooms, others waiting for Andy and our family to emerge hoping to obtain interviews or comments despite the fact that I had informed them that I would be making a statement to them on the steps of the court.

We remained in the courtroom for quite a few minutes after which, as agreed, I, together with other members of the family, went to the steps of Lewes Court and, surrounded by reporters and television cameras, read my statement on behalf of Andy. I thanked everyone for the support they had given us, family, friends and many people who we did not know. Andy particularly thanked Mr Sayers and all his legal team, also the judge. I went on to say, 'It is a pity that we had to go through two trials to get to the end result. Andy never denied what he did. He was prepared to accept punishment for it in whatever way the judge thought appropriate. We fully understand the difficulties surrounding the case. Jacob was extremely ill and going to die but we are not suggesting for one moment that should give carte blanche in any circumstances.'

I concluded my statement by requesting that we now all be left to grieve our loss of Jacob which we had so far been unable to do. I declined to answer any questions, although one television reporter asked me if I thought that the verdict would be seen as a message to all those parents with disabled children that it was all right for them to kill them. I did not reply but I heard my son, Chris, say, 'That is the most disgusting and stupid question I have heard from an experienced member of the media. You should be ashamed of yourself.' Needless to say that exchange was not broadcast.

Mary also made a statement to the press in which she stated that she was 'shocked by the sentence and the message it gives to others'. She was perfectly entitled to her opinion and was raising a moral point in a much more intelligent way than the reporter.

We all then adjourned to the White Hart. It had been agreed that Andy would not be with us when I made the press statement but that he would join us later at the White Hart – not to celebrate but to relax for a few minutes with his family for the first time in seventeen months knowing that his dreadful ordeal was over. The press and television waited for him to emerge from the court and cross the road to the hotel. They took their pictures but he made no comment when asked questions. They followed him but did not enter the White Hart.

The next day a local newspaper printed a quote from a friend of Andy who said that after hearing the verdict he told him, 'My darling little Jacob is looking down on me from above and looking after me.' I think that sums up all our feelings at the time.

All the family knew that there would be great pressure from the press to give them exclusive stories and we discussed at great length the pros and cons of doing so. We did not want to get involved with the popular tabloid newspapers, mainly out of respect for Jacob and because we felt we would have no control over what was printed regardless of what we said. We never wanted to make any monetary gain from what had happened to us.

None of my immediate family received payment for any newspaper articles or interviews and the only interview I gave was to a local newspaper and related to the lessons that could be learnt with the social services etc. from the death of Jacob.

Immediately at the conclusion of the second trial several stories about Andy and Mary's private life appeared in some tabloid and Sunday publications, which can only be described as 'disgusting' and for which the persons responsible were presumably paid large sums of money. What truth there was in those stories I have no idea, I have never discussed it with Andy and I really do not want to know. Andy and Mary's private life involving their social activities was discussed very little during the trials as it was obvious that it had nothing to do with the reasons for Jacob's death.

It is the journalists' job to produce copy that will sell the newspapers that employ – that pay – them. But if only the people who instigate the publication of such stories, which we see every week in our newspapers, would think for just one short moment of what potential damage they might do to children of the families involved, who are undoubtedly going to read the stories at some point in the future: the day must come when those stories, whether true or not, have to be explained. How many of us, including journalists, can honestly say that we have nothing in our lives that we would not want our children to know about? Very few, if any, I suspect.

What a terrible memorial to Jacob are some of the stories that appeared in some of the popular newspapers – how sad it is to know that one day in the years to come George will come upon and read these sordid accounts. It is partly because of those articles that I decided to write this book. I wanted to give a true account of our experience for George and in memory of Jacob.

Once the trial was over, many journalists seemed to do an about-turn. The potential for sensational copy that lay with the trial no longer existed, and it was time for them to move on. But not all did. Even those who had generally been sympathetic up to that time now ripped into Andy and Mary, basically saying that they were unfit, unloving parents, in many cases totally ignoring the evidence that had been given in court.

Of course, not all columnists were of that opinion – Ulrika Johnson and Lorraine Kelly wrote very sympathetic articles in which they said that Andy and Mary should not be condemned for their actions and that we should learn lessons from the case and be much more aware of the pressures parents bringing up disabled children were under.

Two particularly vitriolic pieces were written, however, one of which resulted in me complaining to the Press Complaints Commission.

What I considered to be a very distasteful article was published in the *Sunday Mirror* in which the reporter, Carole Malone, said that Mary 'sounded like an irresponsible tart', and that – referring to her and Andy – 'Neither of this sordid pair should be allowed to bring George up.'

Ms Malone is entitled to her opinion as to what Mary 'sounded' like but making such a statement relating to George's upbringing is inexcusable. With respect – no that's wrong, I have no respect – I suggest that she looks up the definition of the word 'ignorant' – I wonder how many other beliefs and opinions this journalist has based on 'lack of knowledge'. Anything to sell papers, I suppose . . .

The second article I took objection to was written by Fergus Shanahan in the *Sun* newspaper. So much so that I complained to the PCC.

I will not go into the sad, sorry details that Mr Shanahan wrote, just suffice to say that, like Ms Malone, he more or less disregarded facts that had been confirmed in court and then gave his opinion based on ignorance, lack of knowledge – perhaps he too should look in the dictionary.

Describing Andy and Mary he said, 'Pity poor Jacob to have been born to such a couple.' In court Andy was described by a number of witnesses as a 'good father', and Mary as 'an excellent mother'.. The judge herself referred to Mary as 'an experienced and dedicated mother'.

Mr Shanahan further wrote, 'Jacob's death was not a mercy killing. He was not at death's door. He was not in agony.'

He was at death's door, Mr Shanahan; two pathologists said so – even to the point that they would have signed a death certificate had they not have been aware of what Andy had done. The judge emphasized this in her sentencing remarks, while Mr Sayers, QC, said that Jacob 'stood at the gates of his last dreadful journey'. Yes, he was in agony, Mr Shanahan. I knew him, and he choked and nearly died in front of me and my wife a short time before his death. You never met him, you have no idea what his physical condition was like.

The main reason for my complaint though, was the dreadful cartoon/ caricature which appeared with Mr Shanahan's article. It depicted Mary kneeling on the floor wearing a crocodile mask and crying crocodile tears. In the background was little Jacob playing with his toys.

Now, no matter what Mr Shanahan, or anyone else for that matter, thought of Mary and Andy, and no matter what my opinion was of his article, what possible justification could there be for allowing such a disgusting drawing to be printed? Every single human being who knew of the case must surely have had sympathetic feelings about the memory of little Jacob. Everyone it seems, with the exception of Mr Shanahan. I suppose it boosted the sales of his paper though.

Following the exchange of a fair amount of correspondence between myself, the Press Complaints Commission and the *Sun* newspaper during 2006, the matter was finally resolved when the Managing Editor wrote a personal apology and expressed regret that Mr Shanahan's article and cartoon had caused my family and myself further upset. I could have pressed further for a public apology but, knowing that if successful it would have only been a very few lines hidden somewhere in the paper, I felt I had taken the matter far enough and made my point on behalf of Andy, Mary, George and especially Jacob.

In fairness to the *Sun* it should be said that one journalist, Mel Hunter, wrote a very sympathetic piece in August 2004 and included an interview with a couple who have a son with Hunter Syndrome in which they vividly described what it is like to bring him up and face the prospect of him dying. That moving article is reprinted in the next chapter.

As I have said several times, most of the journalists were well-disposed towards us. Bobby Stansfield of the *Daily Mirror* and another journalist kindly sent me a number of letters they had received from the public and the vast majority were very sympathetic towards Andy and Mary. Several were from parents who were struggling to cope with handicapped children and some were giving the message 'there but for the grace of God go I'.

The press interest in Andy and my family gradually decreased, but as long as a year after Andy's conviction I received a call from a journalist asking if I would like to give an interview about how we had all coped and moved on since 2005. I thanked him for his interest but declined the offer.

In addition to the press and media coverage of the case there was massive interest on various websites on the internet, not just in this country but world-wide and I have found it most interesting to read the various opinions. Many subjects were raised, including euthanasia and living and coping with severely handicapped children.

Despite my criticism of the press in some areas, I am grateful to them generally for the courtesy they showed myself and my family. I feel it is so important that we continue to have freedom of the press in this country and I hope that my experiences may help someone who finds themselves in similar circumstances. My advice to them would be to realize that the press can help you or crucify you, to be firm and deal with them in a professional manner, but always be aware of that well-known adage that some journalists adhere to: 'Never let the truth get in the way of a good story'.

Chapter 13
The Moral Question

This chapter is not intended or written as an attempt to exonerate Andy for ending Jacob's life. It is also not my intention to persuade the reader to agree with me about the moral issues which Jacob's death raised and about which I have given great thought. There are still some issues on which I am undecided and continue to try to find an answer that seems logical and acceptable to me. As we grow older I believe that our experiences in life alter our opinions and perceptions of things and we should never be too proud to admit that we have changed our mind or were wrong. I have altered my views twice during my life about the death penalty, for example, and I am still prepared to be persuaded either way.

All I hope to do is to ask the reader to have an open mind when reading of my experiences surrounding Jacob's life and sad death, and perhaps relate some of them to traumas or tragedies they have suffered or heard about in their lives.

Some people, mainly because of strongly held religious beliefs, will never be persuaded to alter their opinions on certain subjects, such as abortion and the taking of life, and provided those beliefs are well thought out then I respect the people who hold them. My only problem with many folk is that their belief is often not based on proven fact or logic – the dictionary definition of belief is 'a principle accepted as true, often without proof'.. I find it very difficult to have complete belief in anything that I cannot prove or find a logical explanation for. If I ask the question of someone 'Why do you believe that?' and they can't give me an answer that indicates some evidence of educated research and thought on their part , then I ask myself 'Is that ignorance?' Ignorance – not bothering to look at, or disregarding, the facts.

That is why I had issues with two or three journalists in their reporting of Andy's case – journalists who expressed their opinions and beliefs having blatantly ignored or evidently not researched the facts.

When considering the moral issue of the right or otherwise of Andy to end his son's life, look at the circumstances, think of your life-experiences, ask yourself what you might have done. Does the expression 'There but for the grace of God go I' apply to you?

I do not believe that one has to condone another person's actions but one should not condemn them out of hand, either, without very good reason and consideration. I do not condone what Andy did but I do not condemn him for it. I can fully understand why he ended Jacob's life, I think he took the right course considering all the circumstances he found himself under, and I will even go so far as to say that I think it was a very remarkable and brave act of love for his son.

Anne and I have never felt we have to forgive Andy for anything, we obviously wish it had not happened, but if he released our poor Jacob from his terrible suffering then we thank him. I do not know if I would have found the courage to have ended my grandson's suffering but I hope, had I found myself under the same circumstances as Andy, that I would have done.

The reason I say I do not condone Andy's act of mercy towards Jacob is because once we 'officially' say and accept that it is all right to end the life of a small child who is suffering from a disability or terminal illness then many of those children would be totally unprotected by law. It would create an extremely dangerous situation that would be totally unacceptable.

I am not talking about euthanasia. That is a separate moral question and involves, generally, older people who understand their situation and request an end to it. It is an offence in this country, but I am in favour of euthanasia provided the law is constructed with important and essential safeguards. Andy, on the other hand, is against it. When he first told me I was surprised but, on reflection, why should I have been? I was equating Jacob's death to euthanasia, which of course it wasn't; it was a mercy killing, not in law because there is no such thing in English law, but in reality.

'Thou shall not kill.' So says the Bible.

Regardless of one's religious beliefs, that rule is pretty basic and accepted in any civilized society throughout the world. But of course one can think of several situations where most people would add a caveat to that order, for example in times of war when being attacked by one's enemy. Of course we have to have basic rules under which to live or society would simply descend into chaos.

Consider this scenario. While Andy was in Iraq or Bosnia he might well have been engaged in a close gunfight when being ambushed by the enemy – he could have seen one of his close friends killed in front of him and he would understandably have had immediate hatred for the killer. Suppose he had then identified the killer and shot him dead, partly for self-preservation, but also as an act of revenge. Then suppose Andy had returned home on leave, seen his dying, suffering son and decided to bring his life to an end.

In this scenario I suggest our morals are challenged somewhat. First, Andy would have deliberately killed someone, who at the time he hated, without a second thought. Nobody would have questioned his actions, at the most there might have been an enquiry and he probably would not have faced a trial. Secondly, Andy has ended the life of someone he loved dearly and as an act of love.

The definition of 'diminished responsibility' is complex, much has been written about it and there are a number of 'stated cases' on the subject – it was discussed at great length at both of Andy's trials. However, isn't it strange that under certain circumstances, such as times of conflict, where a person hates another they can be so enraged as to kill them and the brain's reaction causing them to do it is not questioned – it is not considered 'diminished responsibility', it is acknowledged as normal and acceptable under the circumstances. Where one person can see another whom they love suffering so much that they decide to end their life, the reaction of the brain causing them to take that action is questioned.

We put animals 'out of their misery' – not that I am comparing the value of a human's life with that of an animal – and how many soldiers during wars have seen their comrades lying on the battlefield suffering from terrible injuries and, as a result of their pleading, shot them as an act of mercy? Many I suspect, are witnessed by, or even carried out by, senior officers. But how many have later stood trial for murder or manslaughter on the grounds of 'diminished responsibility'? My research has so far found none. If they ended the life of a comrade at home who was suffering from terrible war injuries and who wanted an end to the pain, then a charge of murder or manslaughter would follow. Are they not both cases of euthanasia, which is illegal?

As described earlier in the book, when Jacob was diagnosed with MPS, Mary was over seven months' pregnant with Henry. She and Andy were given the option of terminating the pregnancy when their unborn son was diagnosed with the same condition. They actually asked the doctors about the legality of such a late termination and were told not to be concerned with that as it was a matter for the medical people. (At present the legal limit is twenty-four weeks.) The sad ending of Henry's life in the womb was carried out legally.

Andrew ended the life of Jacob illegally.

Is there a moral dichotomy in those two events? I am certain there is for some people but not others, depending on one's beliefs.

In saying that I am of course not suggesting it should be legal for a parent to end the life of a child under any circumstances. I am posing the question that, if one agrees morally with the legal ending of life in the womb of a child who, as far as we know is not suffering, how does one square that with the legal ending of a life of a child who is suffering terribly, which at the present time is illegal.

In 1989 Tony Bland, aged twenty-two years, suffered severe brain damage when he was crushed as a result of overcrowding at Hillsborough football ground. Ninety-five people died in that dreadful disaster. Tony went into a coma from which he never recovered and was kept alive on a life-support machine, in hospital, for three years. For much of that time both his parents and the doctors wanted to switch off the machine as he was sadly in a vegetative state and the medical prognosis was that he would never recover and would probably die within five years. They were legally prevented from doing so.

Then, in 1992, a court ruled that artificial feeding by tube is medical treatment which can legally be withdrawn. As a result Tony's life-support machine was switched off, his supply of liquid food and water was withheld and he died within several days, basically from starvation and dehydration and the medical effects that that brought about.

If Jacob had reached a point where he was fed by tube at home and his parents had withdrawn that feeding, causing his death, would they have been charged with murder? One presumes so – but could they have used a defence based on the Tony Bland case?

These kinds of dilemmas highlight the problems facing law-makers, and one realizes that laws may not necessarily tally with one's morals and beliefs, and vice versa.

Altruistic filicide, in which parents kill a child, often with disabilities, claiming death is for the child's good, is more common in this country than one would think, and when it does occur it presents great dilemmas and difficulties for the legal authorities – the police, lawyers, judges, social services and the medical profession – all of whom have to abide by the law as it is laid down, but who inevitably have to consider the moral question when dealing with each case.

There are approximately five recognized categories of altruistic filicide, one of which, for example, is quite common – where a mother is suicidal and kills her children in order that they should not have to live without her.

However, the only category we need concern ourselves with here is, in Andy's case, terminating his son's life believing that it is an act of mercy and to end his suffering. Altruistic filicide, as with mercy killing, is not a statute law in England. Such offences are covered by murder or manslaughter, but Andy and I are now of the opinion that consideration should be given to such acts being a separate offence from murder and manslaughter. In America, although there is not a specific offence of altruistic filicide, there are degrees of murder.

Consider this. Andy was charged with murder to which he pleaded 'not guilty'. From the outset he wanted to plead 'guilty' to manslaughter on the grounds of diminished responsibility but he was not able to do so because he was not charged as such. The judge ultimately offered both juries the option of returning a verdict on manslaughter if they found him not guilty, or were unable to agree, on the murder charge. As we know, the first jury could not agree on either and the second found him guilty of manslaughter due to diminished responsibility.

Now, suppose the first jury had failed to agree and the second jury had found him not guilty of both murder and manslaughter. Then we would have a situation where one person takes another's life, for whatever reason, admits it, wants to plead guilty to it, is prepared to accept punishment but walks free. Or would the Crown be in a position to arraign Andy for manslaughter for which he had already been found not guilty?

Could not this loophole be covered by having on statute the offences of various degrees of murder, one of which could include altruistic filicide?

Following the international press and media coverage of Jacob's death and the subsequent trials, there were hundreds of comments from all over the world placed on the internet and I spent a great deal of time reading them. Some were commenting on the treatment of Andy when he was arrested – being refused bail for instance – but the vast majority were dealing with the moral question of whether Andy had the right to end Jacob's life. Many were from parents of disabled children and it is most interesting to read their views.

Some were outraged at Jacob's death and could never conceive ending the life of their child under any circumstances, no matter how bad their suffering or how stressful life was. Some thought Andy should serve a long term in prison.

In contrast, many had great sympathy for Andy and Mary and some said they had often contemplated ending their own child's suffering.

I have great respect for both points of view, and they surely are held by people who have first-hand experience to validate their opinions.

The dilemma is not helped by such comments as were printed in the *Independent* newspaper about Andy's suspended sentence, which criticized the judge and said, 'The lenient sentence in the case will contribute to the belief that killing a disabled child is not as serious as killing a non-disabled child, since now we can see that such a child has little value in the judicial system or indeed within society.' Such a sweeping statement is, in my opinion inexplicable, and a moment's thought and consideration renders it ridiculous.

For those of us, and I am certainly one, who are morally uncertain of their beliefs regarding euthanasia, I would like to address the terribly difficult question of euthanasia for children. The mere thought of the subject will, I am certain, horrify many and be dismissed out of hand, but I make no apology for raising the question and all I hope is that the reader will give it some balanced thought and maybe come to terms with their moral beliefs a little easier.

For a number of years euthanasia of adults has been carried out by doctors in the Netherlands. A 2002 law regulates the practice whereby the doctor concerned must report the facts of the case to the authorities and, provided the strict protocol can be proved to have been carried out, then no prosecution will follow. Prior to that law there is every reason to believe that in the Netherlands euthanasia was practised, with the consent of relatives, but the facts were often not reported. It is still an offence in that country but the law codified a twenty-year-old convention of not prosecuting doctors who carried out euthanasia. Provided the strict criteria are met in each case, then the doctors involved are not in fear of prosecution.

It is undoubtedly the case in the UK today that euthanasia is practised by some members of the medical profession, with the consent of relatives and the patient, but because it is a criminal offence they are obviously reticent about admitting it.

In the Netherlands since 2006 euthanasia of children has been permitted, including newborns. The ending of a child's life is a criminal offence, but provided consent is given by both parents and all other criteria are met, then the physician will not be prosecuted if they can demonstrate that they acted in an emergency situation. Legally that could become clear if a conflict of duties was present, i.e. the duty to save the life of the child conflicts with the duty to alleviate the child's suffering. In cases of childhood euthanasia that were brought to court in the Netherlands during the 1990s, the courts were convinced that the suffering in the individual cases could only be relieved by the ending of the life, thus accepting the conflict of duties, and that all requirements surrounding the decision to end the child's life were fulfilled.

Since the results of these verdicts were published, it would appear that the Dutch society in general has accepted euthanasia for children as a very exceptional option. However, it should be pointed out that the number of cases of childhood euthanasia per year has remained extremely low and the majority of those cases involved children born with degenerative diseases such as spina bifida and incurable genetic disorders.

The view of those Dutch physicians involved in this very difficult area of medicine seems to be that strict regulation of 'life-shortening medical treatment' is vital in order to monitor the public's view of medical practice. The laws relating to euthanasia, both for adults and children, and the interpretation of them by the courts in the Netherlands, seems to have opened up the debate and it is the opinion of the medical profession that it is better to regulate ethically difficult decisions openly rather than to leave these decisions and the medical practice unknown, not discussed or misunderstood by the general public.

Can we not perhaps learn from the Dutch on this extremely complex and difficult subject?

I am fully aware of the strong arguments against euthanasia for both adults and children and of the possible dangers if a society goes down that road – the likes of the notorious Nazi, Dr Joseph Mengele are often mentioned in that context – but when loving parents and physicians are dealing with terribly ill and dying children one can understand the moral and ethical dilemmas they have to wrestle with.

On 6 August 2004 an article appeared in the *Sun* newspaper, written by Mel Hunter, who later covered Andy's trial. That article included an interview with Steve and Jacqui Home who had a nine-year-old son, Matthew, who suffered from Hunter Syndrome.

The Homes apparently knew Andy, Mary and Jacob through Naomi House Hospice, I am not sure how well, but their interview is a moving and honest account of what it is like to bring up a Hunter boy and their fears for the future. Steve and Jacqui have kindly agreed to allow me to reprint some of the article, which highlights the stress and heartbreak the family have to endure but as one reads their words the love they have for Matthew is the overwhelming message.

Matthew was described by his parents as a 'nightmare baby'. Driving them to distraction with his inability to sleep, his speech was impaired and he found simple tasks a struggle. As with Jacob, many hospital visits and tests followed, resulting in MPS being diagnosed.

Steve says, "Then I went on to the web and got hit by, 'No known cure, life expectancy early teens, very rare,' and so on.

' . . . For the first year I was a total mess.'

Jacqui says, 'I had a year when it was like going through a bereavement – which in a way it was. We knew what Matthew's future was and it felt like we were grieving for it then.

The Homes received invaluable support from the MPS Society, and Christine Lavery in particular.

At the age of around four Matthew hit a plateau when he lost the little speech he had and much of the understanding he had developed. The sign language he had learnt also disappeared.

In the last few months Matthew has been prone to choking fits while drinking, caused by liquid entering his lungs. His parents can't help fearing another downward spiral. Though most of the degeneration has been mental, there are other physical signs of his decline.

He can barely walk and can't get out of bed or feed himself unaided.

But through it all Matthew remains amazingly cheerful.

Steve describes his son: 'He is very smiley, very happy, and he loves animals and things with action. He enjoys horse racing on telly – as they go over the jumps, he goes with them.'

The twenty nights he spends at a hospice each year is the only break the couple get.

Steve says, 'Hunter's changes how you look at everything. As a parent, you start hoping your child will become a brain surgeon Then you find out the news we did and your ambitions change to quite scary things like "I hope he doesn't suffer when he dies"'.

'Knowing he will never go through the emotions which make us is incredibly hard.'

It was the television news which brought the biggest upset last week when Jacqui heard about Jacob Wragg's death.

Once Jacqui's initial shock and sympathy subsided, she was filled with fear for Matthew's future. She says, 'With Jacob being just a year older, you can't help wonder if Matthew will suddenly go downhill. We say in a blasé way that life expectancy is early to mid teens, so we pick a number – fifteen – that's five years away.

'But when someone is ten, and Matthew is a month away from ten himself, we do wonder if something is suddenly going to happen. It is very frightening.'

In Hunter's terms, Matthew is relatively healthy, with a good quality of life.

It means that while in their darkest moments the Homes may question what they would do when that changes, they still feel unable to come up with definite answers. Steve is unable to say whether he would help his child to die. He says, 'I can't answer that, because I'm not there. At the moment, no, it is the last thing on my mind . . .

'I can't condone someone doing that but I can't condemn, either. I think we're actually strong enough that we'd follow things through to the end rather than bring the end forward. I can say that at the moment because I'm not there.'

I have included Mel Hunter's interview with Steve and Jacqui Homes because I believe it illustrates very succinctly how the moral dilemma can arise for some parents who have children with terminal illnesses who are going to die, sometimes in painful and distressing ways. Not that I am suggesting for one moment that all of them have particular thoughts of ending their child's life – far from it. However, when circumstances conspire, and the child is seen to be suffering by the people who love it, it is hardly surprising that occasionally the thought of altruistic filicide will occur and, in some cases, be carried out.

It is interesting when reading the comments of Steve and Jacqui to compare their experience with those of Andy and Mary. It appears that the medical histories of Matthew and Jacob were very similar and typical of Hunter sufferers. What those parents say is, I suggest, more or less identical to what the vast majority of parents who have, or have had, Hunter boys would say when relating their experiences. Andy and Mary certainly would.

No one knows what the future holds for the Homes, but one thing I am sure of is that the 'smiley and happy' Matthew, as Steve describes him, will always be remembered as just that. I know , because Jacob was HAPPY – Jacob could not 'do sad' .

Chapter 14
Lessons to be Learnt

Having dwelt on how Jacob enriched the lives of family and friends, I would like to turn to how Jacob might actually help many more, through the number of lessons I believe are to be learnt from his all too short life and sad death, both practical and moral.

I have already discussed some. There are others though which I believe should be considered.

We have probably the best criminal justice system in the world. It is not corrupt and is generally seen to be fair. However, my experience with the Family Division has given my family and me a very poor opinion of that section of our judicial system. We are not alone in that view, one only has to look at the Fathers for Justice Campaign, for whom I have a great deal of sympathy, to realize that something needs to be done to speed up the process to allow parents access to their children after the break-up of a relationship. Yes, it is sad that partners should use children as pawns but when, as in Andy's application for access to George, one is told by the court that the partner's wishes and feelings are not of paramount importance, then perhaps it is time to reconsider. There is no dispute that of course a child's welfare should be the major factor, but the decision of a court can in the long term greatly affect one partner or the other, and ultimately affect the child's life.

From my experience with our application for access to George, difficult though the task of the family court is, I would like to see less lip-service and a more pragmatic approach. The possibility of opening the family courts to the public and press, as with the criminal courts is, I believe, being considered and that may be a way forward.

Jacob's situation, by its very nature, brought him and his parents into many areas outside their normal family life, bringing into their daily life dealings with social services, the health service, various funding committees, the MPS, the hospice movement and education authorities.

I know these official departments generally carry out their work to the best of their ability, but are often restricted in what they can do, usually because of lack of funds.

I have mentioned the various official authorities, especially the social services. Families who need and ask for backing from social services will invariably be under stress without having to battle every inch of the way because they are often refused, for whatever reason, or given little help. I know the social services themselves work under great pressure and lack sufficient funds but I feel they should acknowledge and admit their failings and not make excuses when things are not done or they are unable to do them – as my wife says, 'There is no such thing as a "problem" – it is a "challenge".' The challenges facing local authorities, especially the lack of provision of services to families caring for children with degenerative and terminal illnesses, were only too well described in the press release issued by Christine Lavery, MBE, Chief Executive of the MPS Society, at the conclusion of the second trial.

Because of the publicity generated by the trials, many parents of Hunter Syndrome children were understandably upset and concerned. So Christine, who attended both trials, issued a press statement on behalf of the Society, as follows:

Press Statement on behalf of the Society for Mucopollysaccharide Diseases

We have heard over the last two weeks many statements about Jacob and how Hunter Disease affected him. Hunter Disease is a complex condition that tragically results in affected children at the severe end of the spectrum losing all skills and dying in childhood.

There is no doubt that Jacob, like a majority of those suffering from MPS, required constant attention and care. Children like Jacob are doubly incontinent, have poor mobility, difficulties in communicating and considerable medical problems.

However, this does not mean that Jacob did not have a right to life. In his own way, Jacob had a quality of life that included going to school, enjoying outings with his family and seeing his friends at Naomi House Children's Hospice.

MPS diseases are tragic and complex. Parents and carers face many issues that are emotionally, as well as physically challenging.

It was abundantly clear in the evidence given that the family felt that their local authority had failed to provide appropriate care and services to them, which ultimately added significantly to the stresses already inherent in caring for a child like Jacob. If there was to be one positive outcome from the tragedy of Jacob it would be that local authorities throughout the land urgently review their provision of services to families caring for children with degenerative, life-limiting conditions, ensuring that resources are appropriate, adequate and timely. There are over 500 MPS families like Jacob's in the UK, many not receiving an adequate level of resources to meet their needs.

In highlighting some of the areas that affected Andy, Mary and Jacob, I hope I have given the reader food for thought, and trust we can move forward in the future. I must say I am not too optimistic though.

There is cause for optimism in other areas, however: I am delighted that there is now a treatment for Hunter Disease. It is the Enzyme Replacement Therapy called Elaprase and in January 2007 it was licensed in Europe as the only treatment for that disease. It should be emphasized that it is not a complete cure for Hunter's, but is designed to replace the missing or deficient enzyme in those affected. Before Elaprase was licensed it was the subject of the largest and longest, placebo-controlled phase II/III trial of a therapy for a Lysosomal storage disease to date.

It should be understood that Enzyme Replacement Therapy is not a cure for Hunter disease and cannot be used if the patient's symptoms are severe. What it does is delay or reduce the various effects the illness has on the organs and limbs, which makes the quality of life much better for the sufferer. It does not appear to have any effect on the deterioration of the brain though.

It is too early to produce any figures on the success of Elaprase but I understand that Dr Ed Wraith and those involved with it are optimistic that its use is a big step forward.

In England all children and young adults with Hunter disease who meet the treatment criteria – not all do – and who want it are on

Elaprase, funded centrally through the National Commissioning Group, Department of Health, thanks in no small part to the work done and representation of Christine Lavery of the MPS Society.

Northern Ireland has followed a similar funding process but in Wales and Scotland the picture is much grimmer for those with Hunter disease. The All Wales Specialist Medicines Group and the Scottish Medicines Consortium have refused to recommend funding in their respective countries and the only option available to those eligible for public funding is through the courts.

Christine Lavery feels this is wrong and is determined to pursue that course for such families.It seems to me like a 'post-code lottery' and cannot be right when dealing with young people's lives. If a drug is available that can make life easier for a sufferer and ultimately their carer, then surely funds should be available for all of them not depending on where they live.

This can best be highlighted by a young patient named Colin who is now receiving the drug He says, 'When I started on Enzyme Replacement Therapy, in the six-minute walk test I could walk sixteen metres. At my six-minute walk test last week I could walk 257 metres and further if I hadn't run out of time. ERT has changed my life.' For the sake of people like Colin let's stop being political and make their life a little easier.

More public funding needs to be made available for research and drugs needed to treat patients with genetic disorders such as Jacob's and Colin's. Our beloved Jacob was possibly born ten years too early and, because of the severity of his disease, he might not have been suitable for ERT if it had been available – we will never know.

The Children's Hospice Movement do tremendous work, but there are far too few hospices and in my opinion they should get more government funding.

Memories of Jacob

When I started writing this book my main objective was to give a fair account of the events surrounding our grandson's death in order that his brother might one day read the story and appreciate what a remarkable effect Jacob had on all of us and the legacy he has left. It was to be, I suppose, a final part of the grieving process for my beloved grandson, but I did not realize the many avenues I would be led down as I wrote. At times I have found myself in tears, stopped writing and sat down with Anne for a cup of coffee. I did not have to explain anything to her, she understood.

But my overall emotion while writing has been one of happiness – although it has been necessary to recall tragic and dark events that have stirred up sad memories they have always been quickly replaced by happy ones. One glance at Jacob's photograph above my desk and I know his smile is telling me 'Happy Jacob, happy Grandad.'

The memory of our beloved Jacob spreads worldwide to the people who knew him – America, South Africa, Germany and even Australia, where our good friends, Nev and Tricia Miles, now live, having settled in Cairns some years ago. They have known Andy since he was very young, and followed the trials closely from the other side of the world and gave us great support. Both strong champions of the Australian Rainforest Foundation, Give a Tree for Life, they planted a tree in memory of Jacob at Jindalba, part of the Northern Queensland National Park and sent us the certificate as confirmation. It was a wonderful gesture and, even in Australia, Jacob won't be forgotten.

I have asked a number of people who knew Jacob what their lasting memories of him are and some have kindly requested that I record them as a tribute to him.

It may seem strange, but I have not included the thoughts and memories of Jacob's daddy and mummy. I have not even talked to them about it. I believe their thoughts and memories of their son are very private and, having both loved him so dearly throughout his life, I doubt if they could truly put their feelings into words, and that should be respected by everyone.

Paul Holden, a reporter for the Sussex newspaper the Argus, has been a friend of Andy for over twenty tears and met Jacob on a number of occasions. Because of his friendship he did not report on the trials. However, at the conclusion, he wrote a deeply personal account of a story that had touched the hearts of many people both nationally and locally. His article appeared in the Argus on 13 December 2005 and, with thanks to that newspaper, also as a tribute to Andy and particularly Jacob, Paul has agreed to allow me to reprint most of his article, which gives another view of Andy's life with Jacob.

> When I learned that Jacob's mum and dad, Andy and Mary, had been arrested, an overwhelming sense of sadness swept over me.
>
> At the time most people would have been unaware of Jacob's illness or the incredible strain caring for that lovely little boy had put on the family.
>
> Mary was released without charge but Andy was charged with murder and spent more than a week on remand in Lewes Prison.
>
> As he languished for twenty-three hours a day in a miserable cell, I cast my mind back almost a decade to the time when Jacob's condition was first diagnosed.
>
> I remembered going to the home of a friend in Findon Valley at Christmas and unexpectedly finding Andy sitting on a chair in the lounge. His head was bowed and he was silently weeping, which took me by surprise, but burned an image on my mind which has stayed with me all these years.
>
> Up to that point I had no idea Jacob was even sick, let alone destined to die before he reached his teens.
>
> Even as Andy, who seemed distraught to the point of despair, tried to explain the doctor's diagnosis, the seriousness of Jacob's condition didn't really sink in.

Friends tried to comfort him but soothing words only prompted the response, 'You have no idea what it is like knowing your child is going to die.'

And, to be frank, we didn't even have the slightest grasp of what he was going through mentally.

Having known Andy since his teens, I was taken aback by this display of raw emotion from a friend who normally kept his feelings to himself.

Prior to that point I had always regarded Andy as one of those who enjoyed a laugh and a drink, as we all did before marriage and mortgages kicked in. While most of us regarded a night out in Brighton as an adventure, Andy was sailing the world on the QE2, having an incredible time. During his travels he even played football for the QE2. against a top Chinese side, cheered on by 80,000 people.

I did not go to school with Andy but whenever I bumped into him we had a beer or a coffee.

After quitting the sea Andy joined the army and eventually the world-famous SAS and went on to serve in war-torn Bosnia.

I knew Mary vaguely, enough to say hello as we passed in the street, but we had never really shared a conversation.

With great reluctance, Andy, who loved the adventure of army life, made the decision to quit and moved back to Worthing.

When Jacob was four or five, I regularly met up with Andy and his son on Saturdays at the Aquarena swimming pool.

The physical signs of Jacob's illness were becoming apparent but within seconds you forgot he had Hunter syndrome and regarded him as just another fun-loving boy.

Andy and I used to laugh out loud as Jacob, who was absolutely fearless and immensely strong, flung himself into the water without a care in the world. As he launched himself from the poolside, Jacob's face was a picture, his eyes burning with excitement and intelligence. He was, on the surface, just like any other boy of his age.

Occasionally I would look after Jacob while Andy would swim to the deep end and back. He would cling on to me and chatter away like any five-year-old.

When I ran a Worthing League football team Andy played in the centre of mid-field for me, always turning up on time and giving 100 per cent.

Andy always enjoyed watching his beloved Southampton and on one occasion we travelled together to a match.

Now and again I would ask how Jacob was. Usually the reply was 'fine' but on one occasion Andy said Jacob was very sick and you could sense he was worried. He expressed the fear that there might soon come a time when Jacob didn't recognize him and that was something that genuinely troubled him.

This was compounded by the fact that Andy and Mary had terminated, late in pregnancy, another Hunter boy, named Henry, who is buried in Hereford.

It is difficult to even begin to imagine what they went through as a couple during this awful time but suffice to say it was a harrowing experience.

Andy, who hoped that Henry could eventually be buried alongside Jacob, was also concerned about what he perceived to be a lack of respite care in Sussex, which could give Mary – generally regarded as a committed, caring mother – a break. He even told me they had difficulty obtaining an adequate allowance of toilet rolls and incontinence pads for Jacob.

That is why both Mary and Andy were great supporters of the Chestnut Tree House Appeal to build a hospice, which is where Jacob's funeral service was held.

The relationship suffered under intense strain and they split up, which seemed inevitable.

Before Andy went to Iraq I saw him and he proudly showed me a photograph of Jacob swimming with dolphins in America. Andy was delighted Jacob had been able to enjoy such an experience and as we parted I told him to take care in Iraq.

The next time I saw Andy was on the television news as he was led into court in handcuffs. His hair was much greyer than before he left for Iraq.

In that very moment my memory flashed back to a broken figure of despair at my pal's Findon Valley home.

There was no question in my mind that Andy ended Jacob's life because he could no longer bear to see his son suffer any longer. And having known Andy for twenty years, and witnessed the torment he has been through, I can say with absolute certainty he loved his little boy.

Uncle Chris, Jacob's 'special' uncle has many memories, while I have memories of the two of them , both obviously so happy, kicking his football in the garden and George annoying Jacob as he tried to run off with the ball! When he came to our house Jacob spent a lot of time watching videos of Chris playing football when he was a boy – in his own way he seemed to idolize him.

Chris says:

"I have so many fond memories of Jacob, it's impossible to single out one single moment, or laugh, or hug or kick-about.

What I remember most about my time spent with Jacob is his indefatigable spirit. I was constantly amazed at how, despite his many physical ailments, he would always greet me with a huge grin, a bear-like hug and a laugh (Jacob always seemed to laugh at me). Even towards the end of his life, when his terrible condition took away his physical abilities, the disease could never take away his joie de vivre.

I always felt we had a special bond. I've used these exact words to describe our relationship many times – because it's something I always believed.

Jacob also taught me to be more grateful for the simple things in life, and that the everyday things that we complain about should always be put in their right perspective. Now, whenever I am faced with what I think is a big challenge or problem, I think of the difficulties he overcame every day and my 'problem' becomes so much easier to deal with.

It's no overstatement to say that Jacob changed the lives of every single person he met.

I miss Jacob terribly, but I know that in my heart he is still with us every day."

Tina and her husband Max saw Jacob fairly regularly during his life and they too have many memories of him.

'I will always remember little Jacob at our wedding with his multi-coloured waistcoat which matched his Dad's – he was such a star on that day,' says Tina. 'Whenever I saw him he would always smile and enjoy himself, particularly when he was in the paddling pool at Mum and Dad's. I'm sure he enjoyed his short life as much as his illness would let him, but it broke my heart towards the end when his health deteriorated so quickly. We all loved him so much and he has had an effect on everyone – I will always love him and never forget him.'

Our eldest son, Steve, was Jacob's godfather and he recalls:

"Jacob and I conquered Germany and the USA together! When I lived with my family in Germany, when he was four years old, Jacob, Andy and Mary spent a holiday with us and in the German restaurants I helped him when he was chattering away to the waiters and keeping the locals entertained. When he was aged five we all spent a great holiday in Florida and he absolutely loved Disneyland – Mickey Mouse didn't say much but that didn't stop Jacob asking numerous questions!

For many years Jacob carried a picture of my son, his cousin Noel, wearing his baseball kit. He took it everywhere with him and when he finally saw him again Jacob got his chance . . . he pushed Noel, fully clothed, into the pool in Florida! He could not stop laughing at that one, and Noel, who understood Jacob's condition, was great with him and saw the funny side of it.

I have so many personal happy memories of Jacob, as do my wife Carmen and my children.

Jacob and 'Uncle Weavie', as he called me, had a lot of fun together.

My godson, my privilege."

On several occasions we took Jacob to barbecues at Anne's sister, Sue, and she says; 'I remember Jacob enjoying himself so much with his cousins, and although several years older than Jacob, Nick, Richard and Holly spent all their time playing with him while he was visiting.

Holly, particularly, loved Jacob so much and we still laugh when we all remember him driving everyone mad banging, probably "attacking" is a better word, Nick's full-size drum kit!

'Jacob was such a lovely little boy, it was so sad that he suffered from Hunter's Syndrome. He was a ray of sunshine when he came to visit us and we will never forget him.'

Anne's brother, Ray, who took Jacob in the helicopter says: "We didn't see Jacob very often but when he was on holiday in Cornwall and he visited us with his parents and Chris he seemed so happy. My children, Garry and Kelly, loved playing with him and he seemed to enjoy himself so much. It was very sad that he had a terminal illness, but we will always have happy memories of him."

Lesley-Anne Lloyd was responsible for fund raising for the building of Chestnut Tree Children's Hospice, knew Jacob well and has fond memories of him. She says:

> "Fundraising is an amazing job! Not only do you get to meet wonderful people who are willing to work extremely hard to raise money but you are also lucky enough to meet the people who benefit from the fundraising. Whilst at Chestnut Tree House I was lucky enough to find both in one family; not only did I work with Bob and Anne and all their lovely children and partners, but I also got to meet Jacob, a happy, fun-loving and charming little boy. I remember going to meet Jacob and was met by a very cheeky chap with the biggest smile you could imagine, of course with his football kit on and a ball underarm! [That image was used on a photograph for a brochure the Hospice used for fundraising.] The whole family worked tirelessly to raise funds, not only as Jacob was using the services, but also for so many other families, to improve their quality of life too. It is often perceived that fundraising is only about money but it isn't, it's about people, it's about families,

it's about the fact that raising money and organizing events sometimes changes the balance on the stress and grief that people bear and it's about children like Jacob, a charming boy that shed a shining light in any room that he entered."

Anne has this special message for Jacob:

"From the minute you were born, you were the 'special one'. Nobody can prepare you for the emotions of your first grandchild. You were so loved and cherished by everyone. All the years we had with you were magic. You responded so much to our love and gave us all such wonderful memories. I remember so well those lovely sunny days we had in our garden when you were in the paddling pool and you loved splashing and throwing water at Grandad and me. During your early years you were encouraged to learn and communicate and those skills stood you in good stead for the deteriorating years. I miss you so much, and never a day goes by when I don't talk to you. All my love and God bless – Nannie."

These tributes are from just a few people who knew Jacob – but since his death he has touched many different people in one way or another – strangers who read about his death, other children with Hunter Syndrome, families with disabled or terminally ill children, charity fundraisers, journalists covering the trial, those in the legal profession, maybe you, the reader, too, the list is endless … who would have thought that the life and death of one little boy could affect so many people from so many walks of life.

At Christmas 2004 Naomi House Hospice held a carol concert at Portsmouth Cathedral, as they alway do, to remember the children from the Hospice who have sadly passed away. I received an invitation and after much thought decided to attend with Tina. Andy, who was still awaiting trial, did not think it right to go and Anne felt the occasion would be too much for her.

The Cathederal was beautifully decorated for Christmas. There was a brass band and choir and a large congregation. Tina and I sat near the back.

The first carol was 'Oh Little Town of Bethlehem' and immediately the choir began to sing I broke down crying. I just lost control of my emotions thinking about our little Jacob who was no longer with us and my mind went back to the nativity play he had performed in at school. Tina put her arm round me and led me away from the congregation. A member of the church guided us to another part of the church where we could see and hear the service and be alone. At the end of the service we lit a candle for Jacob and placed it under the Christmas tree.

I still sometimes wonder whether I should have gone to that service and why I reacted as I did. After all, there were several parents there who had lost children to dreadful terminal illnesses. I suppose the difference was that they were going through a normal grieving process, if there is such a thing, whereas we were not. Jacob's death was expected sometime and if it had happened as we anticipated we would have been able to go through a period of mourning. That never happened, events did not allow it. We were devastated by his passing of course, but immediately we had to cope with the prospect of our son facing life imprisonment.

During the concert a poem was read, the origin of which is uncertain, but is believed to have been written by a thirteen year old girl who had terminal cancer and gave it to her mother just before she died in December 1997. I find it so emotionally moving and it brings tears to my eyes each time I read it. However, I always remind myself that it is a 'happy message' and I am sure Jacob would want us all to look upon it as such – Jacob was happy, Jacob didn't 'do sad.'

My First Christmas in Heaven

I see the countless Christmas trees around the world below,
With tiny lights, like heaven's stars, reflecting in the snow.
The sight is so spectacular, please wipe away the tear,
For I am spending Christmas with Jesus Christ this year.

I hear the many Christmas songs that people hold so dear'
But earthly music can't compare with Christmas choirs up here.
I have no words to tell you, the joy the voices bring,
It is beyond description, to hear the angels sing.

I know how much you miss me, the pain inside you heart,
But I am not so far away, we aren't so far apart.
Be happy for me dear ones, you know I hold so dear:
Be glad I'm spending Christmas with Jesus Christ this year.

I send you each a special gift from my heavenly home above:
I send you each a memory of my undying love.
After all "LOVE" is the gift more precious far than gold:
And always most important in the stories Jesus told.

Please love and keep each other, as my Father said to do,
For I can't count the blessings and love he has for you
So have a merry Christmas and wipe away that tear:
Remember – I'm spending Christmas with Jesus Christ this year.

In 1993 the MPS Society leased an area of land in Sherwood Forest from Nottinghamshire County Council and in October of each year parents and friends who have lost children are invited to plant a tree in their memory.

On 20 October 2006 Andy and I went to the ceremony, Anne unfortunately was unable to attend due to illness.

It was a very moving day for both of us. We first had lunch with Christine Lavery, her husband, members of staff of the MPS Society and a number of families and friends of children who had passed away and had travelled from all over the UK.

We all then proceeded to Sherwood Forest, made famous by the legend of Robin Hood, and went to the MPS area known as Childhood Wood.

After a short non-denominational service and the reading of a beautiful poem, the names of the children whom we were remembering were read out. As the name Jacob Wragg was read, tears filled my eyes, I put my arm around Andy's shoulder and he was obviously moved.

We all then walked the short distance to the planting area where we were given a small oak sapling. Andy planted it and stood in silent thought for few moments – other families did likewise.

Everyone was then given blue and white balloons which we released and watched disappear up into the cloudless sky.

Next to the planting site a commemoration board has been erected bearing the names of all the children who have passed away as a result of one or other of the MPS diseases and had a tree planted in remembrance.

It was good to know that in 2005 Mary and George also planted a tree for Jacob in the Forest. It was a pity that they could not have been with Andy but at the time he was awaiting his second trial. Andy has said that one day he would like to return there with George.

We all have our memories of Jacob but Sherwood Forest is a quiet, peaceful place for us to visit from time to time, to see his tree growing, remember his legacy of happiness and know that he will never be forgotten.

I like to think that the oak sapling Andy planted is a symbol of Jacob's Ladder and as it grows it represents a soul that did not die in 2004, but lives on as a thing of beauty and an example to us all.

Postscript

It hardly seems five years ago that the events I have described in this book took place. All of us have moved on in our lives but none of us will ever forget our beloved Jacob. No day goes by without Anne and me thinking about him. Many things remind us of him and we often talk lovingly about him. I can honestly say that we very rarely think or talk of the sad times – our memories of him invariably cause us to smile or laugh and that is the legacy he has left us.

As mentioned previously in the book, Elaprase an Enzyme Replacement Therapy for Hunter Disease was licensed in Europe in 2007. Christine Lavery of M.P.S. has kindly informed me that it continues to be available to those sufferers who meet the criteria in England and Northern Ireland and I am pleased to say now in Wales. However, the Scottish Medicines Consortium still refuse to recommend the funding of the drug on grounds of health economics. Christine is continuing her legal fight to get them to come into line with the rest of the U.K. Some things never change ! She is pleased to report though that parents of children who first received Elaprase five years ago as part of the clinical trial report a halting in the degenerative process of the disease and a much improved quality of life for their children. Unfortunately the drug is not a cure for Hunter Disease and has shown no benefit to children or adults with severe progressive degenerative brain disorder.

Andy is a sales manager working for an I.T. Company and seems to be enjoying it despite the current difficult economic climate. He spends quite a lot of his spare time fishing which I am sure he finds quite therapeutic. George lives with his Mum and her partner but Andy now sees him on a regular basis and often brings him to us for lunch.

George is now eleven years old and is growing up fast. He is a handsome looking young lad, physically very well developed and strong for his age. He loves sport, just like his Dad and supports Chelsea as did Jacob. He plays both football and cricket for local boys' teams and Andy and I often watch him play. Andy bought George a set of golf clubs and they love going to the golf range .They also go swimming together. He seems to be getting on well at school and although Andy sometimes talks about Jacob with him it will obviously be some time before he can put into perspective the events which so effected his young life in 2004. George is polite and well mannered and shows his love for us – he is a credit to his Mum and Dad. I have every confidence for his future and believe he will be successful in whatever path he follows in life.

July 2009